BLUEPRINTS:
A PROBLEM NOTEBOOK

FUNDAMENTALS

OF

FINANCIAL

MANAGEMENT:

CONCISE THIRD EDITION

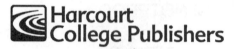
Harcourt College Publishers

Where Learning Comes to Life

TECHNOLOGY
Technology is changing the learning experience, by increasing the power of your textbook and other learning materials; by allowing you to access more information, more quickly; and by bringing a wider array of choices in your course and content information sources.

Harcourt College Publishers has developed the most comprehensive Web sites, e-books, and electronic learning materials on the market to help you use technology to achieve your goals.

PARTNERS IN LEARNING
Harcourt partners with other companies to make technology work for you and to supply the learning resources you want and need. More importantly, Harcourt and its partners provide avenues to help you reduce your research time of numerous information sources.

Harcourt College Publishers and its partners offer increased opportunities to enhance your learning resources and address your learning style. With quick access to chapter-specific Web sites and e-books . . . from interactive study materials to quizzing, testing, and career advice . . . Harcourt and its partners bring learning to life.

Harcourt's partnership with Digital:Convergence™ brings :CRQ™ technology and the :CueCat™ reader to you and allows Harcourt to provide you with a complete and dynamic list of resources designed to help you achieve your learning goals. Just swipe the cue to view a list of Harcourt's partners and Harcourt's print and electronic learning solutions.

.C 62 00 00 00 00 00 26 20

http://www.harcourtcollege.com/partners/

BLUEPRINTS:
A PROBLEM NOTEBOOK

FUNDAMENTALS

OF

FINANCIAL

MANAGEMENT:

CONCISE THIRD EDITION

EUGENE F. BRIGHAM
AND
JOEL F. HOUSTON

University of Florida

Harcourt College Publishers

Fort Worth   Philadelphia   San Diego   New York   Orlando   Austin   San Antonio
Toronto   Montreal   London   Sydney   Tokyo

Address for Domestic Orders
Harcourt College Publishers, 6277 Sea Harbor Drive, Orlando, FL 32887-6777
800-782-4479

Address for International Orders
International Customer Service
Harcourt, Inc., 6277 Sea Harbor Drive, Orlando, FL 32887-6777
407-345-3800
(fax) 407-345-4060
(e-mail) hbintl@harcourt.com

Address for Editorial Correspondence
Harcourt College Publishers, 301 Commerce Street, Suite 3700, Fort Worth, TX 76102

Web Site Address
http://www.harcourtcollege.com

Printed in the United States of America

1 2 3 4 5 6 7 8 9 0   202   9 8 7 6 5 4 3 2 1

Harcourt College Publishers

PREFACE

Blueprints has become an integral part of the material we provide to students. At the University of Florida, we teach a large class, with upwards of 1,000 students each semester. This large class size forces us to lecture, even though we prefer discussion-oriented classes. To get the students more involved, we have developed a set of integrated cases that cover the key points in each chapter and which we use as the basis for our lectures. For our classes, we use the computer slide show to present the material that is summarized in each integrated case. Early on, students began asking us to make copies of the slides available to them. We did so, and that improved the class considerably. With paper copies of the slides, students could focus on what was being said in the lecture without having to copy things down for later review. *Blueprints* includes a copy of each integrated case, copies of the slides, space to write down additional notes, and extra exam-type problems for each chapter.

We consider the current version quite complete. However, the <u>optimal</u> product varies from instructor to instructor, depending on how the class is conducted. Therefore, instructors are encouraged to modify *Blueprints* to suit their own styles and interests. For example, if one covers chapters in a different order, or does not cover certain chapters, or covers only part of some chapters, or has additional materials not covered in the text, or anything else, the *Blueprints* chapters can be rearranged, added to or subtracted from, or modified in any other way.

Students always want copies of old exams. Also, we have review sessions, conducted by TAs, and those sessions are devoted to working exam-type problems. So, we have included a number of exam-type problems at the end of each *Blueprints* chapter. Students work them on their own or else go to review sessions where the TAs work them. The solutions for these exam-type problems are provided at the end of the last *Blueprints* chapter.

Instructors can use *Blueprints* in conjunction with the computer slide show, which is based on the integrated cases. Also, we frequently use the blackboard, both to explain the calculations that lie behind some of the numbers and to provide different examples. Our students end up with lots of marginal notes that clarify various points.

One thing has become crystal clear over the years—the best lecture notes, and materials related thereto, are instructor-specific. It is difficult to use someone else's notes verbatim. However, there is no point in reinventing the wheel, and if the *Blueprints* wheel fits a particular instructor's wagon, he or she might do well to use it, spending time adapting it to his or her own style and coverage rather than taking the time to develop lectures notes de novo. Therefore, you are encouraged to look over the *Blueprints* package, decide if and how you might use it, and then go to it. If you are like us, you will change things from semester to semester—there is no such thing as static optimality!

If you do use the package, and find some modifications that work well for you, we would very much appreciate hearing from you—your modifications might well help us and others.

Eugene F. Brigham
Joel F. Houston

P.O. Box 117168
Department of Finance, Insurance, and Real Estate
Warrington College of Business
University of Florida
Gainesville, Florida 32611-7168

April 2001

SUGGESTIONS FOR STUDENTS USING BLUEPRINTS

1. Read the textbook chapter first, going through the entire chapter rapidly. Don't expect to understand everything on this first reading, but do try to get a good idea of what the chapter covers, the key terms, and the like. <u>It is useful to read the chapter before the first lecture on it.</u>

2. You could also read the *Blueprints* chapter material before class, but that is not necessary.

3. *Blueprints* was designed as the basis for a lecture—the most important material in each chapter is covered, and the material most likely to give you trouble is emphasized. As your instructor goes through *Blueprints*, you should (1) see what we regard as the most important material and (2) get a better feel for how to think about issues and work relevant problems.

4. You could read *Blueprints*, in connection with the text, and get a reasonably good idea of what is going on in the course. However, the real value of *Blueprints* is as a vehicle to help the class lecture make more sense and to help you get a good set of notes. In class, your instructor will discuss various points raised in *Blueprints* and elaborate on different issues. Also, he or she will explain how formulas are used, where data in tables come from, and the like. <u>You will end up with lots of marginal notes on your copy if you use *Blueprints* as it is supposed to be used.</u> Indeed, these marginal notes will constitute your class notes.

BLUEPRINTS

Table of Contents

CHAPTER	1	An Overview of Financial Management	1 - 1
CHAPTER	2	Financial Statements, Cash Flow, and Taxes	2 - 1
CHAPTER	3	Analysis of Financial Statements	3 - 1
CHAPTER	4	Financial Planning and Forecasting	4 - 1
CHAPTER	5	The Financial Environment: Markets, Institutions, and Interest Rates	5 - 1
CHAPTER	6	Risk and Rates of Return	6 - 1
CHAPTER	7	Time Value of Money	7 - 1
CHAPTER	8	Bonds and Their Valuation	8 - 1
CHAPTER	9	Stocks and Their Valuation	9 - 1
CHAPTER	10	The Cost of Capital	10 - 1
CHAPTER	11	The Basics of Capital Budgeting	11 - 1
CHAPTER	12	Cash Flow Estimation and Risk Analysis	12 - 1
CHAPTER	13	Capital Structure and Leverage	13 - 1
CHAPTER	14	Distributions to Shareholders: Dividends and Share Repurchases	14 - 1
CHAPTER	15	Working Capital Management	15 – 1
CHAPTER	16	Multinational Financial Management	16 - 1

1-2 Kato Summers opened Take a Dive 17 years ago; the store is located in Malibu, California, and sells surfing-related equipment. Today, Take a Dive has 50 employees including Kato and his daughter Amber, who works part time in the store to help pay for her college education.

Kato's business has boomed in recent years, and he is looking for new ways to take advantage of his increasing business opportunities. Although Kato's formal business training is limited, Amber will soon graduate with a degree in finance. Kato has offered her the opportunity to join the business as a full-fledged partner. Amber is interested, but she is also considering other career opportunities in finance.

Right now, Amber is leaning toward staying with the family business, partly because she thinks it faces a number of interesting challenges and opportunities. Amber is particularly interested in further expanding the business and then incorporating it. Kato is intrigued by her ideas, but he is also concerned that her plans might change the way in which he does business. In particular, Kato has a strong commitment to social activism, and he has always tried to strike a balance between work and pleasure. He is worried that these goals will be compromised if the company incorporates and brings in outside shareholders.

Amber and Kato plan to take a long weekend off to sit down and think about all of these issues. Amber, who is highly organized, has outlined a series of questions for them to address:

a. What kinds of career opportunities are open to finance majors?

b. What are the primary responsibilities of a corporate financial staff?

c. What are the most important financial management issues today?

d. (1) What are the alternative forms of business organization?

   (2) What are their advantages and disadvantages?

e. What is the primary goal of the corporation?

   (1) Do firms have any responsibilities to society at large?

   (2) Is stock price maximization good or bad for society?

   (3) Should firms behave ethically?

f. What is an agency relationship?

    (1) What agency relationships exist within a corporation?

    (2) What mechanisms exist to influence managers to act in shareholders' best interests?

    (3) Should shareholders (through managers) take actions that are detrimental to bondholders?

g. Is maximizing stock price the same thing as maximizing profit?

h. What factors affect stock prices?

i. What factors affect the level and riskiness of cash flows?

1 - 1

CHAPTER 1
An Overview of Financial Management

- Career opportunities
- Issues of the new millennium
- Forms of business organization
- Goals of the corporation
- Agency relationships

---

1 - 2

Career Opportunities in Finance

- Money and capital markets
- Investments
- Financial management

---

1 - 3

Responsibilities of the Financial Staff

- Forecasting and planning
- Investment and financing decisions
- Coordination and control
- Transactions in the financial markets
- Managing risk

Financial Management Issues of the New Millennium

- Use of computers and electronic transfers of information
- The globalization of business

Percentage of Revenue and Net Income from Overseas Operations for 10 Well-Known Corporations, 1999

Company	Percentage of Revenue Originated Overseas	Percentage of Net Income Generated Overseas
Chase Manhattan	23.9	21.9
Coca-Cola	61.2	65.1
Exxon Mobil	71.8	62.7
General Electric	31.7	22.8
General Motors	26.3	55.3
IBM	57.5	49.6
McDonald's	61.6	60.9
Merck	21.6	43.4
Minn. Mining & Mfg.	52.1	27.2
Walt Disney	15.4	16.6

Alternative Forms of Business Organization

- Sole proprietorship
- Partnership
- Corporation

Sole Proprietorship

- **Advantages:**
  - Ease of formation
  - Subject to few regulations
  - No corporate income taxes
- **Disadvantages:**
  - Limited life
  - Unlimited liability
  - Difficult to raise capital

Partnership

- A partnership has roughly the same advantages and disadvantages as a sole proprietorship.

Corporation

- **Advantages:**
  - Unlimited life
  - Easy transfer of ownership
  - Limited liability
  - Ease of raising capital
- **Disadvantages:**
  - Double taxation
  - Cost of set-up and report filing

Goals of the Corporation

- The primary goal is shareholder wealth maximization, which translates to maximizing stock price.
  - Do firms have any responsibilities to society at large?
  - Is stock price maximization good or bad for society?
  - Should firms behave ethically?

Agency Relationships

- An agency relationship exists whenever a principal hires an agent to act on their behalf.
- Within a corporation, agency relationships exist between:
  - Shareholders and managers
  - Shareholders and creditors

Shareholders versus Managers

- Managers are naturally inclined to act in their own best interests.
- But the following factors affect managerial behavior:
  - Managerial compensation plans
  - Direct intervention by shareholders
  - The threat of firing
  - The threat of takeover

Shareholders versus Creditors

- Shareholders (through managers) could take risky actions to maximize stock price, but are detrimental to creditors.

- In the long run, such actions will raise the cost of debt and ultimately lower stock price.

Does profit maximization equal stock price maximization?

No, there is generally a high correlation between EPS, cash flow, and stock price, but today's stock price relies not only on current earnings, but future earnings and cash flows.

Some actions may increase earnings, yet cause stock price to decrease (and vice versa).

Factors that Affect Stock Price

- Projected cash flows to shareholders
- Timing of the cash flow stream
- Riskiness of the cash flows

Factors that Affect the Level and Riskiness of Cash Flows

- Decisions made by financial managers:
  - Investment decisions
  - Financing decisions (the relative use of debt financing)
  - Dividend policy decisions
- The external environment

_____

_____

_____

_____

_____

_____

_____

EXAM-TYPE PROBLEMS

1-1. Which of the following statements is most correct?

   a. Agency is the main method of transferring ownership interest in a corporation.

   b. The corporation is a legal entity created by the state and is a direct extension of the legal status of its owners and managers, that is, the owners and managers are the corporation.

   c. Unlimited liability and limited life are two key advantages of the corporate form over other forms of business organization.

   d. Due in large part to limited liability and ease of ownership transfer, corporations have less trouble raising money in financial markets than other organizational forms.

   e. The stockholders of the corporation are insulated by limited legal liability, and the legal status of the corporation protects the firm's managers from civil and criminal charges arising from business operations.

1-2. Which of the following statements is most correct?

   a. The proper goal of the financial manager should be to maximize the firm's expected cash flow, because this will add the most wealth to each of the individual shareholders (owners) of the firm.

   b. One way to state the decision framework most useful for carrying out the firm's objective is as follows: "The financial manager should seek that combination of assets, liabilities, and capital which will generate the largest expected projected after-tax income over the relevant time horizon."

   c. The riskiness inherent in a firm's earnings per share (EPS) depends on the characteristics of the projects the firm selects, which means it depends upon the firm's assets, but EPS does not depend on the manner in which those assets are financed.

   d. Since large, publicly-owned firms are controlled by their management teams, and typically, ownership is widely dispersed, managers have great freedom in managing the firm. Managers may operate in stockholders' best interests, but they may also operate in their own personal best interests. As long as managers stay within the law, there simply aren't any effective controls over managerial decisions in such situations.

   e. Agency problems exist between stockholders and managers and between stockholders (through managers) and creditors.

2-26 Donna Jamison, a 1996 graduate of the University of Florida with four years of banking experience, was recently brought in as assistant to the chairman of the board of D'Leon Inc., a small food producer that operates in north Florida and whose specialty is high-quality pecan and other nut products sold in the snack-foods market. D'Leon's president, Al Watkins, decided in 2000 to undertake a major expansion and to "go national" in competition with Frito-Lay, Eagle, and other major snack-food companies. Watkins felt that D'Leon's products were of a higher quality than the competition's, that this quality differential would enable it to charge a premium price, and that the end result would be greatly increased sales, profits, and stock price.

The company doubled its plant capacity, opened new sales offices outside its home territory, and launched an expensive advertising campaign. D'Leon's results were not satisfactory, to put it mildly. Its board of directors, which consisted of its president and vice-president plus its major stockholders (who were all local business people), was most upset when directors learned how the expansion was going. Suppliers were being paid late and were unhappy, and the bank was complaining about the deteriorating situation and threatening to cut off credit. As a result, Watkins was informed that changes would have to be made, and quickly, or he would be fired. Also, at the board's insistence Donna Jamison was brought in and given the job of assistant to Fred Campo, a retired banker who was D'Leon's chairman and largest stockholder. Campo agreed to give up a few of his golfing days and to help nurse the company back to health, with Jamison's help.

Jamison began by gathering the financial statements and other data given in Tables IC2-1, IC2-2, IC2-3, and IC2-4. Assume that you are Jamison's assistant, and you must help her answer the following questions for Campo. (Note: We will continue with this case in Chapter 3, and you will feel more comfortable with the analysis there, but answering these questions will help prepare you for Chapter 3. Provide clear explanations, not just yes or no answers!)

TABLE IC2-1. Balance Sheets

	2001	2000
Assets:		
Cash	$ 7,282	$ 57,600
Accounts receivable	632,160	351,200
Inventories	1,287,360	715,200
Total current assets	$1,926,802	$1,124,000
Gross fixed assets	1,202,950	491,000
Less accumulated depreciation	263,160	146,200
Net fixed assets	$ 939,790	$ 344,800
Total assets	$2,866,592	$1,468,800
Liabilities and equity:		
Accounts payable	$ 524,160	$ 145,600
Notes payable	636,808	200,000
Accruals	489,600	136,000
Total current liabilities	$1,650,568	$ 481,600
Long-term debt	723,432	323,432
Common stock (100,000 shares)	460,000	460,000
Retained earnings	32,592	203,768
Total equity	$ 492,592	$ 663,768
Total liabilities and equity	$2,866,592	$1,468,800

TABLE IC2-2. Income Statements

	2001	2000
Sales	$6,034,000	$3,432,000
Cost of goods sold	5,528,000	2,864,000
Other expenses	519,988	358,672
Total operating costs excluding depreciation	$6,047,988	$3,222,672
EBITDA	($ 13,988)	$ 209,328
Depreciation	116,960	18,900
EBIT	($ 130,948)	$ 190,428
Interest expense	136,012	43,828
EBT	($ 266,960)	$ 146,600
Taxes (40%)	(106,784)[a]	58,640
Net income	($ 160,176)	$ 87,960
EPS	($1.602)	$0.880
DPS	$0.110	$0.220
Book value per share	$4.926	$6.638
Stock price	$2.25	$8.500
Shares outstanding	100,000	100,000
Tax rate	40.00%	40.00%
Lease payments	40,000	40,000
Sinking fund payments	0	0

Note:
[a] The firm had sufficient taxable income in 1999 and 2000 to obtain its full tax refund in 2001.

TABLE IC2-3. Statement of Retained Earnings, 2001

Balance of retained earnings, 12/31/00	$203,768
Add: Net income, 2001	(160,176)
Less: Dividends paid	(11,000)
Balance of retained earnings, 12/31/01	$ 32,592

TABLE IC2-4. Statement of Cash Flows, 2001

OPERATING ACTIVITIES
Net income	($ 160,176)
Additions (Sources of Cash):	
Depreciation	116,960
Increase in accounts payable	378,560
Increase in accruals	353,600
Subtractions (Uses of Cash):	
Increase in accounts receivable	(280,960)
Increase in inventories	(572,160)
Net cash provided by operating activities	($ 164,176)

LONG-TERM INVESTING ACTIVITIES
Cash used to acquire fixed assets	($ 711,950)

FINANCING ACTIVITIES
Increase in notes payable	436,808
Increase in long-term debt	400,000
Payment of cash dividends	(11,000)
Net cash provided by financing activities	$ 825,808

Sum: Net decrease in cash	($ 50,318)
Plus: Cash at beginning of year	57,600
Cash at end of year	$ 7,282

a. What effect did the expansion have on sales, net operating profit after taxes (NOPAT), net operating working capital (NOWC), total investor-supplied operating capital, and net income?

b. What effect did the company's expansion have on its net cash flow, operating cash flow, and free cash flow?

c. Jamison also has asked you to estimate D'Leon's EVA. She estimates that the after-tax cost of capital was 10 percent in 2000 and 13 percent in 2001.

d. Looking at D'Leon's stock price today, would you conclude that the expansion increased or decreased MVA?

e. D'Leon purchases materials on 30-day terms, meaning that it is supposed to pay for purchases within 30 days of receipt. Judging from its 2001 balance sheet, do you think D'Leon pays suppliers on time? Explain. If not, what problems might this lead to?

f. D'Leon spends money for labor, materials, and fixed assets (depreciation) to make products, and still more money to sell those products. Then, it makes sales that result in receivables, which eventually result in cash inflows. Does it appear that D'Leon's sales price exceeds its costs per unit sold? How does this affect the cash balance?

g. Suppose D'Leon's sales manager told the sales staff to start offering 60-day credit terms rather than the 30-day terms now being offered. D'Leon's competitors react by offering similar terms, so sales remain constant. What effect would this have on the cash account? How would the cash account be affected if sales doubled as a result of the credit policy change?

h. Can you imagine a situation in which the sales price exceeds the cost of producing and selling a unit of output, yet a dramatic increase in sales volume causes the cash balance to decline?

i. Did D'Leon finance its expansion program with internally generated funds (additions to retained earnings plus depreciation) or with external capital? How does the choice of financing affect the company's financial strength?

j. Refer to Tables IC2-2 and IC2-4. Suppose D'Leon broke even in 2001 in the sense that sales revenues equaled total operating costs plus interest charges. Would the asset expansion have caused the company to experience a cash shortage that required it to raise external capital?

k. If D'Leon started depreciating fixed assets over 7 years rather than 10 years, would that affect (1) the physical stock of assets, (2) the balance sheet account for fixed assets, (3) the company's reported net income, and (4) its cash position? Assume the same depreciation method is used for stockholder reporting and for tax calculations, and the accounting change has no effect on assets' physical lives.

l. Explain how earnings per share, dividends per share, and book value per share are calculated, and what they mean. Why does the market price per share *not* equal the book value per share?

m. The 2001 income statement shows negative taxes, that is, a tax credit. Given the tax refund received in 2001, what can you conclude about the amount of taxes paid in the previous 2 years?

n. Working with Jamison has required you to put in a lot of overtime, so you have had very little time to spend on your private finances. It's now April 1, and you have only two weeks left to file your income tax return. You have managed to get all the information together that you will need to complete your return. D'Leon paid you a salary of $45,000, and you received $3,000 in dividends from common stock that you own. You are single, so your personal exemption is $2,800, and your itemized deductions are $5,150.

   (1) On the basis of the information above and the April 2001 individual tax rate schedule, what is your tax liability?

   (2) What are your marginal and average tax rates?

o. Assume that a corporation has $100,000 of taxable income from operations plus $5,000 of interest income and $10,000 of dividend income. What is the company's tax liability?

p. Assume that after paying your personal income tax as calculated in Part n, you have $5,000 to invest. You have narrowed your investment choices down to California bonds with a yield of 7 percent or equally risky Exxon Mobil bonds with a yield of 10 percent. Which one should you choose and why? At what marginal tax rate would you be indifferent to the choice between California and Exxon Mobil bonds?

CHAPTER 2
Financial Statements, Cash Flow, and Taxes

- Balance sheet
- Income statement
- Statement of cash flows
- Accounting income vs. cash flow
- MVA and EVA
- Personal taxes
- Corporate taxes

---

2 - 2

Balance Sheet: Assets

	2001	2000
Cash	7,282	57,600
AR	632,160	351,200
Inventories	1,287,360	715,200
Total CA	1,926,802	1,124,000
Gross FA	1,202,950	491,000
Less: Deprec.	263,160	146,200
Net FA	939,790	344,800
Total Assets	2,866,592	1,468,800

---

2 - 3

Liabilities and Equity

	2001	2000
Accts payable	524,160	145,600
Notes payable	636,808	200,000
Accruals	489,600	136,000
Total CL	1,650,568	481,600
Long-term debt	723,432	323,432
Common stock	460,000	460,000
Retained earnings	32,592	203,768
Total equity	492,592	663,768
Total L&E	2,866,592	1,468,800

Income Statement

	2001	2000
Sales	6,034,000	3,432,000
COGS	5,528,000	2,864,000
Other expenses	519,988	358,672
EBITDA	(13,988)	209,328
Depr. & Amort.	116,960	18,900
EBIT	(130,948)	190,428
Interest exp.	136,012	43,828
EBT	(266,960)	146,600
Taxes (40%)	(106,784)	58,640
Net income	(160,176)	87,960

Other Data

	2001	2000
No. of shares	100,000	100,000
EPS	($1.602)	$0.88
DPS	$0.110	$0.22
Stock price	$2.25	$8.50
Lease pmts	$40,000	$40,000

Statement of Retained Earnings (2001)

Balance of retained earnings, 12/31/00	$203,768
Add: Net income, 2001	(160,176)
Less: Dividends paid	(11,000)
Balance of retained earnings, 12/31/01	$32,592

Statement of Cash Flows (2001)

OPERATING ACTIVITIES
Net income	(160,176)

Add (Sources of cash):
Depreciation	116,960
Increase in A/P	378,560
Increase in accruals	353,600

Subtract (Uses of cash):
Increase in A/R	(280,960)
Increase in inventories	(572,160)

Net cash provided by ops.	**(164,176)**

L-T INVESTING ACTIVITIES
Investment in fixed assets	(711,950)

FINANCING ACTIVITIES
Increase in notes payable	436,808
Increase in long-term debt	400,000
Payment of cash dividends	(11,000)
Net cash from financing	825,808

NET CHANGE IN CASH	**(50,318)**

Plus: Cash at beginning of year	57,600
Cash at end of year	7,282

What can you conclude about D'Leon's financial condition from its statement of CFs?

- Net cash from operations = -$164,176, mainly because of negative NI.

- The firm borrowed $825,808 to meet its cash requirements.

- Even after borrowing, the cash account fell by $50,318.

Did the expansion create additional net operating profit after taxes (NOPAT)?

$$NOPAT = EBIT(1 - \text{Tax rate}).$$

$$NOPAT_{01} = -\$130,948(1 - 0.4)$$
$$= -\$130,948(0.6)$$
$$= -\$78,569.$$

$$NOPAT_{00} = \$114,257.$$

What effect did the expansion have on net operating working capital (NOWC)?

$$NOWC = \text{Current assets} - \text{Non-interest bearing CL}.$$

$$NOWC_{01} = (\$7,282 + \$632,160 + \$1,287,360)$$
$$- (\$524,160 + \$489,600)$$
$$= \$913,042.$$

$$NOWC_{00} = \$842,400.$$

What effect did the expansion have on capital used in operations?

$$\text{Operating capital} = NOWC + \text{Net fixed assets}.$$

$$\text{Operating capital}_{01} = \$913,042 + \$939,790$$
$$= \$1,852,832.$$

$$\text{Operating capital}_{00} = \$1,187,200.$$

What is your initial assessment of the expansion's effect on operations?

	2001	2000
Sales	$6,034,000	$3,432,000
NOPAT	($78,569)	$114,257
NOWC	$913,042	$842,400
Operating capital	$1,852,832	$1,187,200
Net Income	($160,176)	$87,960

What effect did the company's expansion have on its net cash flow and operating cash flow?

$NCF_{01} = NI + DEP = (\$160,176) + \$116,960$
$= (\$43,216).$

$NCF_{00} = \$87,960 + \$18,900 = \$106,860.$

$OCF_{01} = NOPAT + DEP$
$= (\$78,569) + \$116,960$
$= \$38,391.$

$OCF_{00} = \$114,257 + \$18,900$
$= \$133,157.$

What was the free cash flow (FCF) for 2001?

FCF = OCF – Gross capital investment.
-OR-
FCF = NOPAT – Net capital investment
$= -\$78,569 – (\$1,852,832 – \$1,187,200)$
$= -\$78,569 – \$665,632$
$= -\$744,201.$

Is negative free cash flow always a bad sign?

Economic Value Added (EVA)

$$EVA = \frac{\text{Operating Income}}{\text{After Tax}} - \frac{\text{After-Tax}}{\text{Capital Costs}}$$

$$= \frac{\text{Funds Available}}{\text{to Investors}} - \frac{\text{Cost of}}{\text{Capital Used}}$$

$$= \text{NOPAT} - \frac{\text{After-Tax}}{\text{Cost of Capital}}$$

EVA Concepts

- In order to generate positive EVA, a firm has to more than just cover operating costs. It must also provide a return to those who have provided the firm with capital.
- EVA takes into account the total cost of capital, which includes the cost of equity.

What is the company's EVA? Assume the firm's after-tax percentage cost of capital was 10% in 2000 and 13% in 2001.

EVA_{01} = NOPAT − (A-T cost of capital)(Capital)
= -$78,569 − (0.13)($1,852,832)
= -$78,569 − $240,868
= -$319,437.

EVA_{00} = $114,257 − (0.10)($1,187,200)
= $114,257 − $118,720
= -$4,463.

Would you conclude that the expansion increased or decreased MVA?

$$MVA = \frac{\text{Market value}}{\text{of equity}} - \frac{\text{Equity capital}}{\text{supplied}}$$

During the last year stock price has decreased 73%, so market value of equity has declined. Consequently, MVA has declined.

Leading Creators of Wealth in the U.S. Market Value Added in 2000

Company	Market Value Added
General Electric	$502,307 million
Microsoft	$388,922 million
Cisco Systems	$377,883 million
Intel	$281,832 million
Pfizer	$260,984 million
Merck	$193,348 million
EMC	$191,904 million
Oracle	$180,885 million
American Int'l Group	$177,982 million
Wal-Mart Stores	$177,450 million

Does D'Leon pay its suppliers on time?

- Probably not.
- A/P increased 260% over the past year, while sales increased by only 76%.
- If this continues, suppliers may cut off D'Leon's trade credit.

---

2 - 22

Does it appear that D'Leon's sales price exceeds its cost per unit sold?

- No, the negative NOPAT and decline in cash position shows that D'Leon is spending more on its operations than it is taking in.

---

2 - 23

What effect would each of these actions have on D'Leon's cash account?

1. The company offers 60-day credit terms. The improved terms are matched by its competitors, so sales remain constant.

   - A/R would ↑
   - Cash would ↓

---

2 - 24

2. Sales double as a result of the change in credit terms.

   - Short run: Inventory and fixed assets ↑ to meet increased sales. A/R ↑, Cash ↓. Company may have to seek additional financing.
   - Long-run: Collections increase and the company's cash position would improve.

How did D'Leon finance its expansion?

- D'Leon financed its expansion with external capital.
- D'Leon issued long-term debt which reduced its financial strength and flexibility.

Would D'Leon have required external capital if they had broken even in 2001 (Net Income = 0)?

- YES, the company would still have to finance its increase in assets. Looking to the Statement of Cash Flows, we see that the firm made an investment of $711,950 in net fixed assets. Therefore, they would have needed to raise additional funds.

What happens if D'Leon depreciates its fixed assets over 7 years (as opposed to the current 10 years)?

- No effect on physical assets.
- Fixed assets on balance sheet would decline.
- Net income would decline.
- Tax payments would decline.
- Cash position would improve.

D'Leon received a tax credit of $106,784 in 2001.

- This suggests the company paid at least $106,784 in taxes during the past 2 years.

- If D'Leon's payments over the past 2 years were less than $106,784 the firm would have had to carry forward the amount of its loss that was not carried back.

- If the firm did not receive a full refund its cash position would be even worse.

INCOME TAXES

April 2001 Single Individual Tax Rates

Taxable Income	Tax on Base	Rate*
0 - 26,250	0	15%
26,250 - 63,550	3,937.50	28%
63,550 - 132,600	14,381.50	31%
132,600 - 288,350	35,787.00	36%
Over 288,350	91,857.00	39.6%

*Plus this percentage on the amount over the bracket base.

Assume your salary is $45,000, and you received $3,000 in dividends. You are single, so your personal exemption is $2,800 and your itemized deductions are $5,150.

On the basis of the information above and the April 2001 tax rate schedule, what is your tax liability?

Calculation of Taxable Income

Salary	$45,000
Dividends	3,000
Personal exemptions	(2,800)
Deductions	(5,150)
Taxable Income	$40,050

40,050 - 26,250

⇧

- Tax Liability:

TL = $3,937.50 + 0.28($13,800)

= $7,801.50 ≈ $7,802.

- Marginal Tax Rate = 28%.
- Average Tax Rate:

Tax rate = $\frac{\$7,802}{\$40,050}$ = 19.48% ≈ 19.5%.

January 2001 Corporate Tax Rates

Taxable Income	Tax on Base	Rate*
0 - 50,000	0	15%
50,000 - 75,000	7,500	25%
75,000 - 100,000	13,750	34%
100,000 - 335,000	22,250	39%
...	...	...
Over 18.3M	6.4M	35%

*Plus this percentage on the amount over the bracket base.

Assume a corporation has $100,000 of taxable income from operations, $5,000 of interest income, and $10,000 of dividend income.

What's its tax liability?

Operating income	$100,000
Interest income	5,000
Taxable dividend income	3,000*
Taxable income	$108,000

Tax = $22,250 + 0.39 ($8,000)
= $25,370.

*Dividends – Exclusion
= $10,000 – 0.7($10,000) = $3,000.

Taxable vs. Tax-Exempt Bonds

State and local government bonds (munis) are generally exempt from federal taxes.

- Exxon Mobil bonds at 10% vs. California muni bonds at 7%.
- T = Tax rate = 28%.
- After-tax interest income:

Exxon Mobil = 0.10($5,000) −
$$0.10(\$5,000)(0.28)$$
$$= 0.10(\$5,000)(0.72) = \$360.$$
$$CAL = 0.07(\$5,000) - 0 = \$350.$$

At what tax rate would you be indifferent to muni vs. corp?

Solve for T in this equation:

$$\text{Muni yield} = \text{Corp Yield}(1 - T)$$
$$7.00\% = 10.0\%(1 - T)$$
$$T = 30.0\%.$$

Implications

- If $T > 30\%$, buy tax-exempt munis.
- If $T < 30\%$, buy corporate bonds.
- Only high income people should buy munis.

EXAM-TYPE PROBLEMS

2-1.   Which of the following statements is most correct?

a. In order to avoid double taxation and to escape the frequently higher tax rate applied to capital gains, stockholders generally prefer to have corporations pay dividends rather than to retain their earnings and reinvest the money in the business. Thus, earnings should be retained only if the firm needs capital very badly and would have difficulty raising it from external sources.

b. Under our current tax laws, when investors pay taxes on their dividend income, they are being subjected to a form of double taxation.

c. The fact that a percentage of the interest received by one corporation, which is paid by another corporation, is excluded from taxable income has encouraged firms to use more debt financing relative to equity financing.

d. If the tax laws stated that $0.50 out of every $1.00 of interest paid by a corporation was allowed as a tax-deductible expense, this would probably encourage companies to use more debt financing than they presently do, other things held constant.

e. Statements b and d are correct.

2-2.   Solarcell Corporation has $20,000 that it plans to invest in marketable securities. It is choosing between AT&T bonds that yield 11 percent, State of Florida muni bonds that yield 8 percent, and AT&T preferred stock with a dividend yield of 9 percent. Solarcell's corporate tax rate is 40 percent, and 70 percent of the preferred stock dividends it receives are tax exempt. Assuming that the investments are equally risky and that Solarcell chooses strictly on the basis of after-tax returns, which security should be selected? Answer by giving the after-tax rate of return on the highest yielding security. (8%)

2-3.   Purcell Corporation has operating income (EBIT) of $1,250,000. The company's depreciation expense is $300,000. Purcell is 100 percent equity financed, and it faces a 40 percent tax rate. In addition, the firm's net investment in operating capital is $500,000.

a. What is the company's net income? ($750,000)

b. What is its net cash flow? ($1,050,000)

c. What is its operating cash flow? ($1,050,000)

d. What is its net operating profit after taxes (NOPAT)? ($750,000)

e. What is its free cash flow (FCF)? ($250,000)

3-22　Part I of this case, presented in Chapter 2, discussed the situation that D'Leon Inc., a regional snack-foods producer, was in after an expansion program. D'Leon had increased plant capacity and undertaken a major marketing campaign in an attempt to "go national." Thus far, sales have not been up to the forecasted level, costs have been higher than were projected, and a large loss occurred in 2001 rather than the expected profit. As a result, its managers, directors, and investors are concerned about the firm's survival.

Donna Jamison was brought in as assistant to Fred Campo, D'Leon's chairman, who had the task of getting the company back into a sound financial position. D'Leon's 2000 and 2001 balance sheets and income statements, together with projections for 2002, are given in Tables IC3-1 and IC3-2. In addition, Table IC3-3 gives the company's 2000 and 2001 financial ratios, together with industry average data. The 2002 projected financial statement data represent Jamison's and Campo's best guess for 2002 results, assuming that some new financing is arranged to get the company "over the hump."

Jamison examined monthly data for 2001 (not given in the case), and she detected an improving pattern during the year. Monthly sales were rising, costs were falling, and large losses in the early months had turned to a small profit by December. Thus, the annual data look somewhat worse than final monthly data. Also, it appears to be taking longer for the advertising program to get the message across, for the new sales offices to generate sales, and for the new manufacturing facilities to operate efficiently. In other words, the lags between spending money and deriving benefits were longer than D'Leon's managers had anticipated. For these reasons, Jamison and Campo see hope for the company—provided it can survive in the short run.

Jamison must prepare an analysis of where the company is now, what it must do to regain its financial health, and what actions should be taken. Your assignment is to help her answer the following questions. Provide clear explanations, not yes or no answers.

TABLE IC3-1. Balance Sheets

	2002E	2001	2000
Assets:			
Cash	$ 85,632	$ 7,282	$ 57,600
Accounts receivable	878,000	632,160	351,200
Inventories	1,716,480	1,287,360	715,200
Total current assets	$2,680,112	$1,926,802	$1,124,000
Gross fixed assets	1,197,160	1,202,950	491,000
Less accumulated depreciation	380,120	263,160	146,200
Net fixed assets	$ 817,040	$ 939,790	$ 344,800
Total assets	$3,497,152	$2,866,592	$1,468,800
Liabilities and Equity:			
Accounts payable	$ 436,800	$ 524,160	$ 145,600
Notes payable	300,000	636,808	200,000
Accruals	408,000	489,600	136,000
Total current liabilities	$1,144,800	$1,650,568	$ 481,600
Long-term debt	400,000	723,432	323,432
Common stock	1,721,176	460,000	460,000
Retained earnings	231,176	32,592	203,768
Total equity	$1,952,352	$ 492,592	$ 663,768
Total liabilities and equity	$3,497,152	$2,866,592	$1,468,800

Note: "E" indicates estimated. The 2002 data are forecasts.

TABLE IC3-2. Income Statements

	2002E	2001	2000
Sales	$7,035,600	$6,034,000	$3,432,000
Cost of goods sold	5,875,992	5,528,000	2,864,000
Other expenses	550,000	519,988	358,672
Total operating costs excluding depreciation	$6,425,992	$6,047,988	$3,222,672
EBITDA	$ 609,608	($ 13,988)	$ 209,328
Depreciation	116,960	116,960	18,900
EBIT	$ 492,648	($ 130,948)	$ 190,428
Interest expense	70,008	136,012	43,828
EBT	$ 422,640	($ 266,960)	$ 146,600
Taxes (40%)	169,056	(106,784)[a]	58,640
Net income	$ 253,584	($ 160,176)	$ 87,960
EPS	$1.014	($1.602)	$0.880
DPS	$0.220	$0.110	$0.220
Book value per share	$7.809	$4.926	$6.638
Stock price	$12.17	$2.250	$8.500
Shares outstanding	250,000	100,000	100,000
Tax rate	40.00%	40.00%	40.00%
Lease payments	40,000	40,000	40,000
Sinking fund payments	0	0	0

Note: "E" indicates estimated. The 2002 data are forecasts.

[a]The firm had sufficient taxable income in 1999 and 2000 to obtain its full tax refund in 2001.

TABLE IC3-3. Ratio Analysis

	2002E	2001	2000	Industry Average
Current		1.2×	2.3×	2.7×
Quick		0.4×	0.8×	1.0×
Inventory turnover		4.7×	4.8×	6.1×
Days sales outstanding (DSO)[a]		38.2	37.4	32.0
Fixed assets turnover		6.4×	10.0×	7.0×
Total assets turnover		2.1×	2.3×	2.6×
Debt ratio		82.8%	54.8%	50.0%
TIE		-1.0×	4.3×	6.2×
EBITDA coverage		0.1×	3.0×	8.0×
Profit margin		-2.7%	2.6%	3.5%
Basic earning power		-4.6%	13.0%	19.1%
ROA		-5.6%	6.0%	9.1%
ROE		-32.5%	13.3%	18.2%
Price/earnings		-1.4×	9.7×	14.2×
Price/cash flow		-5.2×	8.0×	11.0×
Market/book		0.5×	1.3×	2.4×
Book value per share		$4.93	$6.64	n.a.

Note: "E" indicates estimated. The 2002 data are forecasts.
[a] Calculation is based on a 365-day year.

a. Why are ratios useful? What are the five major categories of ratios?

b. Calculate D'Leon's 2002 current and quick ratios based on the projected balance sheet and income statement data. What can you say about the company's liquidity position in 2000, 2001, and as projected for 2002? We often think of ratios as being useful (1) to managers to help run the business, (2) to bankers for credit analysis, and (3) to stockholders for stock valuation. Would these different types of analysts have an equal interest in the liquidity ratios?

c. Calculate the 2002 inventory turnover, days sales outstanding (DSO), fixed assets turnover, and total assets turnover. How does D'Leon's utilization of assets stack up against other firms in its industry?

d. Calculate the 2002 debt, times-interest-earned, and EBITDA coverage ratios. How does D'Leon compare with the industry with respect to financial leverage? What can you conclude from these ratios?

e. Calculate the 2002 profit margin, basic earning power (BEP), return on assets (ROA), and return on equity (ROE). What can you say about these ratios?

f. Calculate the 2002 price/earnings ratio, price/cash flow ratio, and market/book ratio. Do these ratios indicate that investors are expected to have a high or low opinion of the company?

g. Use the extended Du Pont equation to provide a summary and overview of D'Leon's financial condition as projected for 2002. What are the firm's major strengths and weaknesses?

h. Use the following simplified 2002 balance sheet to show, in general terms, how an improvement in the DSO would tend to affect the stock price. For example, if the company could improve its collection procedures and thereby lower its DSO from 45.6 days to the 32-day industry average without affecting sales, how would that change "ripple through" the financial statements (shown in thousands below) and influence the stock price?

Accounts receivable	$ 878	Debt	$1,545
Other current assets	1,802		
Net fixed assets	817	Equity	1,952
Total assets	$3,497	Liabilities plus equity	$3,497

i. Does it appear that inventories could be adjusted, and, if so, how should that adjustment affect D'Leon's profitability and stock price?

j. In 2001, the company paid its suppliers much later than the due dates, and it was not maintaining financial ratios at levels called for in its bank loan agreements. Therefore, suppliers could cut the company off, and its bank could refuse to renew the loan when it comes due in 90 days. On the basis of data provided, would you, as a credit manager, continue to sell to D'Leon on credit? (You could demand cash on delivery, that is, sell on terms of COD, but that might cause D'Leon to stop buying from your company.) Similarly, if you were the bank loan officer, would you recommend renewing the loan or demand its repayment? Would your actions be influenced if, in early 2002, D'Leon showed you its 2002 projections plus proof that it was going to raise over $1.2 million of new equity capital?

k. In hindsight, what should D'Leon have done back in 2000?

l. What are some potential problems and limitations of financial ratio analysis?

m. What are some qualitative factors analysts should consider when evaluating a company's likely future financial performance?

CHAPTER 3
Analysis of Financial Statements

- Ratio analysis
- Du Pont system
- Effects of improving ratios
- Limitations of ratio analysis
- Qualitative factors

Balance Sheet: Assets

	2002E	2001
Cash	85,632	7,282
AR	878,000	632,160
Inventories	1,716,480	1,287,360
Total CA	2,680,112	1,926,802
Gross FA	1,197,160	1,202,950
Less: Deprec.	380,120	263,160
Net FA	817,040	939,790
Total assets	3,497,152	2,866,592

Liabilities and Equity

	2002E	2001
Accounts payable	436,800	524,160
Notes payable	300,000	636,808
Accruals	408,000	489,600
Total CL	1,144,800	1,650,568
Long-term debt	400,000	723,432
Common stock	1,721,176	460,000
Retained earnings	231,176	32,592
Total equity	1,952,352	492,592
Total L & E	3,497,152	2,866,592

Income Statement

	2002E	2001
Sales	7,035,600	6,034,000
COGS	5,875,992	5,528,000
Other expenses	550,000	519,988
EBITDA	609,608	(13,988)
Depreciation	116,960	116,960
EBIT	492,648	(130,948)
Interest exp.	70,008	136,012
EBT	422,640	(266,960)
Taxes (40%)	169,056	(106,784)
Net income	253,584	(160,176)

Other Data

	2002E	2001
Shares out.	250,000	100,000
EPS	$1.014	($1.602)
DPS	$0.220	$0.110
Stock price	$12.17	$2.25
Lease pmts	$40,000	$40,000

Why are ratios useful?

- Standardize numbers; facilitate comparisons
- Used to highlight weaknesses and strengths

What are the five major categories of ratios, and what questions do they answer?

■ **Liquidity:** Can we make required payments?

■ **Asset management:** Right amount of assets vs. sales?

■ **Debt management:** Right mix of debt and equity?

■ **Profitability:** Do sales prices exceed unit costs, and are sales high enough as reflected in PM, ROE, and ROA?

■ **Market value:** Do investors like what they see as reflected in P/E and M/B ratios?

Calculate D'Leon's forecasted current and quick ratios for 2002.

$$CR_{02} = \frac{CA}{CL} = \frac{\$2,680}{\$1,145} = 2.34x.$$

$$QR_{02} = \frac{CA - Inv.}{CL}$$

$$= \frac{\$2,680 - \$1,716}{\$1,145} = 0.84x.$$

Comments on CR and QR

	2002	2001	2000	Ind.
CR	2.34x	1.2x	2.3x	2.7x
QR	0.84x	0.4x	0.8x	1.0x

- Expected to improve but still below the industry average.
- Liquidity position is weak.

What is the inventory turnover ratio vs. the industry average?

$$\text{Inv. turnover} = \frac{\text{Sales}}{\text{Inventories}}$$

$$= \frac{\$7,036}{\$1,716} = 4.10x.$$

	2002	2001	2000	Ind.
Inv. T.	4.1x	4.7x	4.8x	6.1x

Comments on Inventory Turnover

- Inventory turnover is below industry average.
- D'Leon might have old inventory, or its control might be poor.
- No improvement is currently forecasted.

DSO is the average number of days after making a sale before receiving cash.

$$DSO = \frac{Receivables}{Average\ sales\ per\ day}$$

$$= \frac{Receivables}{Sales/365} = \frac{\$878}{\$7,036/365} = 45.6.$$

Appraisal of DSO

	2002	2001	2000	Ind.
DSO	45.6	38.2	37.4	32.0

- D'Leon collects too slowly, and is getting worse.
- D'Leon has a poor credit policy.

F.A. and T.A. Turnover versus Industry Average

$$\frac{Fixed\ assets}{turnover} = \frac{Sales}{Net\ fixed\ assets}$$

$$= \frac{\$7,036}{\$817} = 8.61x.$$

$$\frac{Total\ assets}{turnover} = \frac{Sales}{Total\ assets}$$

$$= \frac{\$7,036}{\$3,497} = 2.01x.$$

	2002	2001	2000	Ind.
FA TO	8.6x	6.4x	10.0x	7.0x
TA TO	2.0x	2.1x	2.3x	2.6x

- FA turnover projected to exceed industry average. Good.

- TA turnover not up to industry average. Caused by excessive current assets (A/R and Inv.)

Calculate the debt ratio, TIE, and EBITDA coverage ratios.

$$\text{Debt ratio} = \frac{\text{Total debt}}{\text{Total assets}}$$

$$= \frac{\$1,145 + \$400}{\$3,497} = 44.2\%.$$

$$\text{TIE} = \frac{\text{EBIT}}{\text{Int. expense}}$$

$$= \frac{\$492.6}{\$70} = 7.0x.$$

EBITDA coverage =

$$\frac{\text{EBITDA + Lease payments (in cash)}}{\text{Interest expense} + \text{Lease pmt.} + \text{Principal repayments}}$$

$$= \frac{\$609.6 + \$40}{\$70 + \$40 + \$0} = 5.9x.$$

How do the debt management ratios compare with industry averages?

	2002	2001	2000	Ind.
D/A	44.2%	82.8%	54.8%	50.0%
TIE	7.0x	-1.0x	4.3x	6.2x
EBITDA coverage	5.9x	0.1x	3.0x	8.0x

D/A and TIE are better than industry average but EBITDA still below industry average.

Profit margin vs. industry average?

$$P.M. = \frac{NI}{Sales} = \frac{\$253.6}{\$7,036} = 3.6\%.$$

	2002	2001	2000	Ind.
P.M.	3.6%	-2.7%	2.6%	3.5%

Very bad in 2001, but projected to exceed industry average in 2002. Looking good.

BEP vs. industry average?

$$BEP = \frac{EBIT}{Total\ assets}$$

$$= \frac{\$492.6}{\$3,497} = 14.1\%.$$

	2002	2001	2000	Ind.
BEP	14.1%	-4.6%	13.0%	19.1%

- BEP removes effect of taxes and financial leverage. Useful for comparison.
- Projected to be below average.
- Room for improvement.

Return on Assets

$$ROA = \frac{\text{Net income}}{\text{Total assets}}$$

$$= \frac{\$253.6}{\$3,497} = 7.3\%.$$

$$ROE = \frac{\text{Net income}}{\text{Common equity}}$$

$$= \frac{\$253.6}{\$1,952} = 13.0\%.$$

	2002	2001	2000	Ind.
ROA	7.3%	-5.6%	6.0%	9.1%
ROE	13.0%	-32.5%	13.3%	18.2%

Both below average but improving.

Effects of Debt on ROA and ROE

- ROA is lowered by debt--interest lowers NI, which also lowers ROA = NI/Assets.

- But use of debt lowers equity, hence could raise ROE = NI/Equity.

Typical Industry Average P/E Ratios

Industry	P/E ratio
Banking	16.58
Computer Software Services	84.28
Drug	43.89
Electric Utilities (Eastern U.S.)	25.28
Internet Services*	326.53
Semiconductors	85.44
Steel	12.38
Tobacco	11.07
Water Utilities	22.30

* Because many Internet companies have negative earnings and no P/E, there was only a small sample of Internet companies.

$$\text{CF per share} = \frac{\text{NI + Depr.}}{\text{Shares out.}}$$

$$= \frac{\$253.6 + \$117.0}{250} = \$1.48.$$

$$\text{P/CF} = \frac{\text{Price per share}}{\text{Cash flow per share}}$$

$$= \frac{\$12.17}{\$1.48} = 8.21x.$$

$$\text{BVPS} = \frac{\text{Com. equity}}{\text{Shares out.}}$$

$$= \frac{\$1,952}{250} = \$7.81.$$

$$\text{M/B} = \frac{\text{Mkt. price per share}}{\text{Book value per share}}$$

$$= \frac{\$12.17}{\$7.81} = 1.56x.$$

	2002	2001	2000	Ind.
P/E	12.0x	-1.4x	9.7x	14.2x
P/CF	8.21x	-5.2x	8.0x	11.0x
M/B	1.56x	0.5x	1.3x	2.4x

- P/E: How much investors will pay for $1 of earnings. High is good.
- P/CF: How much investors will pay for $1 of cash flow. High is good.
- M/B: How much paid for $1 of BV. Higher is better.
- P/E and M/B are high if ROE is high, risk is low.

$$\left(\begin{array}{c}\text{Profit}\\\text{margin}\end{array}\right)\left(\begin{array}{c}\text{TA}\\\text{turnover}\end{array}\right)\left(\begin{array}{c}\text{Equity}\\\text{multiplier}\end{array}\right) = \text{ROE}$$

$$\frac{\text{NI}}{\text{Sales}} \times \frac{\text{Sales}}{\text{TA}} \times \frac{\text{TA}}{\text{CE}} = \text{ROE}.$$

Year				
2000	2.6%	x	2.3	x	2.2 = 13.3%
2001	-2.7%	x	2.1	x	5.8 = -32.5%
2002	3.6%	x	2.0	x	1.8 = 13.0%
Ind.	3.5%	x	2.6	x	2.0 = 18.2%

The Du Pont system focuses on:

- Expense control (P.M.)
- Asset utilization (TATO)
- Debt utilization (Eq. Mult.)

It shows how these factors combine to determine the ROE.

Simplified D'Leon Data

A/R	878	Debt	1,545
Other CA	1,802	Equity	1,952
Net FA	817		
Total assets	$3,497	L&E	$3,497

$$\frac{Sales}{day} = \frac{\$7,035,600}{365} = \$19,275.62.$$

Q. How would reducing DSO to 32 days affect the company?

Effect of reducing DSO from 45.6 days to 32 days:

Old A/R = 19,275.62 x 45.6 = 878,000

New A/R = 19,275.62 x 32.0 = 616,820

Cash freed up: 261,180

Initially shows up as additional cash.

New Balance Sheet

Added cash	$ 261	Debt	$1,545
A/R	617	Equity	1,952
Other CA	1,802		
Net FA	817		
Total assets	$3,497	Total L&E	$3,497

What could be done with the new
cash? Effect on stock price and risk?

Potential use of freed up cash

- Repurchase stock
- Expand business
- Reduce debt
- All these actions would improve
  stock price.

What are some potential problems and limitations of financial ratio analysis?

- Comparison with industry averages
  is difficult if the firm operates many
  different divisions.
- "Average" performance not
  necessarily good.
- Seasonal factors can distort ratios.

- ■ "Window dressing" techniques can make statements and ratios look better.
- ■ Different operating and accounting practices distort comparisons.
- ■ Sometimes hard to tell if a ratio is "good" or "bad."
- ■ Difficult to tell whether company is, on balance, in strong or weak position.

What are some qualitative factors analysts should consider when evaluating a company's likely future financial performance?

- ■ Are the company's revenues tied to 1 key customer, product, or supplier?
- ■ What percentage of the company's business is generated overseas?
- ■ Competition
- ■ Future prospects
- ■ Legal and regulatory environment

EXAM-TYPE PROBLEMS

3-1.   Automotive Supply's ROE last year was only 2 percent, but its new owner has developed an operating plan designed to improve things. The new plan calls for a total debt ratio of 70 percent, which will result in interest charges of $500 per year. Management projects an EBIT of $2,000 on sales of $20,000, and it expects to have a total assets turnover ratio of 2.5. Under these conditions, the average tax rate will be 30 percent. If the changes are made, what return on equity will Automotive earn? (43.75%)

3-2.   Capital Garden Supply (CGS) recently hired a new chief financial officer, Louise Johnston, who was brought in and charged with raising the firm's profitability. CGS has sales of $5 million, a profit margin of 5 percent, and the following balance sheet:

Cash	$ 250,000	A/P	$	750,000
Receivables	2,250,000	Other C.L.		500,000
Inventories	1,750,000	Long-term debt		2,250,000
Net fixed assets	3,250,000	Common equity		4,000,000
Total assets	$7,500,000	Total L/E		$7,500,000

a. Ms. Johnston thinks that receivables are too high, and that they can be lowered to the point where the firm's DSO is equal to the industry average, 60 days, without affecting either sales or net income. If receivables are reduced so as to lower the DSO to 60 days (365-day basis), and if the funds generated are used to reduce common equity (stock can be repurchased at book value), and if no other changes occur, by how much will the ROE change? (+3.47%)

b. Suppose we wanted to modify this problem and use it on an exam, i.e., to create a new problem that you have not seen to test your knowledge of this general type of problem. How would your answer change under each of the following conditions:

(1) Double all dollar amounts. (+3.47%)

(2) Set the target DSO at 70 days. (+2.98%)

(3) State that the target is to achieve a receivables turnover (Sales/Receivables) of 6×. (+3.43%)

(4) State that the company has 250,000 shares of stock outstanding, and ask how much the original change would increase EPS. (+$0.56)

(5) Change part 4 to state that the stock was selling for twice book value, so common equity would not be reduced on a dollar-for-dollar basis. (+$0.22)

c. Now explain how we could have set the problem up to have you focus on changing inventory or fixed assets, or using the funds generated to retire debt,

---

or how the original problem could have stated that the company needed *more* inventory and would finance them with new common equity, or with new debt.

3-3.   Which of the following statements is most correct?

a. If two firms pay the same interest rate on their debt and have the same rate of return on assets, and if that ROA is positive, the firm with the *higher* debt ratio will also have a higher rate of return on common equity.

b. One of the problems of ratio analysis is that the relationships are subject to manipulation. For example, we know that if we use some of our cash to pay off some of our current liabilities, the current ratio will always increase, especially if the current ratio is weak initially.

c. Generally, firms with high profit margins have high asset turnover ratios, and firms with low profit margins have low turnover ratios; this result is exactly as predicted by the extended Du Pont equation.

d. Firms A and B have identical earnings and identical dividend payout ratios. If Firm A's growth rate is higher than that of Firm B, Firm A's P/E ratio must be greater than Firm B's P/E ratio.

e. None of the above statements is correct.

3-4.   Alumbat Corporation has $800,000 of debt outstanding, and it pays an interest rate of 10 percent annually on its bank loan. Alumbat's annual sales are $3,200,000; its average tax rate is 40 percent; and its net profit margin on sales is 6 percent. If the company does not maintain a TIE ratio of at least 4 times, its bank will refuse to renew its loan, and bankruptcy will result. What is Alumbat's current TIE ratio? (5×)

3-5.   Austin & Company has a debt ratio of 0.5, a total assets turnover ratio of 0.25, and a profit margin of 10 percent. The Board of Directors is unhappy with the current return on equity (ROE), and they think it could be doubled. This could be accomplished (1) by increasing the profit margin to 12 percent, and (2) by increasing debt utilization. Total assets turnover will not change. What new debt ratio, along with the new 12 percent profit margin, would be required to double the ROE? (70%)

3-6.   Jecko Enterprises has an ROA of 12.5 percent, a 3 percent profit margin, and a return on equity equal to 16 percent.

a. What is the company's total assets turnover? (4.167×)

b. What is the firm's equity multiplier? (1.28)

c. What is the firm's debt ratio? Assume the firm has no preferred stock. (22%)

4-19   Sue Wilson, the new financial manager of New World Chemicals (NWC), a California producer of specialized chemicals for use in fruit orchards, must prepare a financial forecast for 2002. NWC's 2001 sales were $2 billion, and the marketing department is forecasting a 25 percent increase for 2002. Wilson thinks the company was operating at full capacity in 2001, but she is not sure about this. The 2001 financial statements, plus some other data, are given in Table IC4-1.

Table IC4-1. Financial Statements and Other Data on NWC
(Millions of Dollars)

A. 2001 Balance Sheet

Cash and securities	$ 20	Accounts payable and accruals	$100
Accounts receivable	240	Notes payable	100
Inventories	240	Total current liabilities	$200
Total current assets	$ 500	Long-term debt	100
Net fixed assets	500	Common stock	500
		Retained earnings	200
Total assets	$1,000	Total liabilities and equity	$1,000

B. 2001 Income Statement

Sales	$2,000.00
Less: Variable costs	1,200.00
Fixed costs	700.00
Earnings before interest and taxes (EBIT)	$ 100.00
Interest	16.00
Earnings before taxes (EBT)	$ 84.00
Taxes (40%)	33.60
Net income	$ 50.40
Dividends (30%)	$ 15.12
Addition to retained earnings	$ 35.28

C. Key ratios

	NWC	Industry	Comment
Basic earning power	10.00%	20.00%	
Profit margin	2.52	4.00	
Return on equity	7.20	15.60	
Days sales outstanding (365 days)	43.80 days	32.00 days	
Inventory turnover	8.33×	11.00×	
Fixed assets turnover	4.00	5.00	
Total assets turnover	2.00	2.50	
Debt/assets	30.00%	36.00%	
Times interest earned	6.25×	9.40×	
Current ratio	2.50	3.00	
Payout ratio	30.00%	30.00%	

Assume that you were recently hired as Wilson's assistant, and your first major task is to help her develop the forecast. She asked you to begin by answering the following set of questions.

a. Assume (1) that NWC was operating at full capacity in 2001 with respect to all assets, (2) that all assets must grow proportionally with sales, (3) that accounts payable and accruals will also grow in proportion to sales, and (4) that the 2001 profit margin and dividend payout will be maintained. Under these conditions, what will the company's financial requirements be for the coming year? Use the AFN equation to answer this question.

b. Now estimate the 2002 financial requirements using the projected financial statement approach. Disregard the assumptions in part a, and now assume (1) that each type of asset, as well as payables, accruals, and fixed and variable costs, grow in proportion to sales; (2) that NWC was operating at full capacity; (3) that the payout ratio is held constant at 30 percent; and (4) that external funds needed are financed 50 percent by notes payable and 50 percent by long-term debt. (No new common stock will be issued.)

c. Why do the two methods produce somewhat different AFN forecasts? Which method provides the more accurate forecast?

d. Calculate NWC's forecasted ratios, and compare them with the company's 2001 ratios and with the industry averages. How does NWC compare with the average firm in its industry, and is the company expected to improve during the coming year?

e. Calculate NWC's free cash flow for 2002.

f. Suppose you now learn that NWC's 2001 receivables and inventories were in line with required levels, given the firm's credit and inventory policies, but that excess capacity existed with regard to fixed assets. Specifically, fixed assets were operated at only 75 percent of capacity.

   (1) What level of sales could have existed in 2001 with the available fixed assets? What would the fixed assets-to-sales ratio have been if NWC had been operating at full capacity?

   (2) How would the existence of excess capacity in fixed assets affect the additional funds needed during 2002?

g. Without actually working out the numbers, how would you expect the ratios to change in the situation where excess capacity in fixed assets exists? Explain your reasoning.

h. On the basis of comparisons between NWC's days sales outstanding (DSO) and inventory turnover ratios with the industry average figures, does it appear that NWC is operating efficiently with respect to its inventories and accounts receivable? If the company were able to bring these ratios into line with the industry averages, what effect would this have on its AFN and its financial ratios? (Note: Inventories and receivables will be discussed in detail in Chapter 15.)

i. The relationship between sales and the various types of assets is important in financial forecasting. The financial statement method, under the assumption that each asset item grows proportionally with sales, leads to an AFN forecast that is reasonably close to the forecast using the AFN equation. Explain how each of the following factors would affect the accuracy of financial forecasts based on the AFN equation: (1) excess capacity; (2) base stocks of assets, such as shoes in a shoe store; (3) economies of scale in the use of assets; and (4) lumpy assets.

j. (1) How could regression analysis be used to detect the presence of the situations described above and then to improve the financial forecasts? Plot a graph of the following data, which is for a typical well-managed company in NWC's industry to illustrate your answer.

Year	Sales	Inventories
1999	$1,280	$118
2000	1,600	138
2001	2,000	162
2002E	2,500	192

(2) On the same graph that plots the above data, draw a line that shows how the regression line would have to appear to justify the use of the AFN formula and the projected financial statement forecasting method. As a part of your answer, show the growth rate in inventories that results from a 10 percent increase in sales from a sales level of (a) $200 and (b) $2,000 based on both the actual regression line and a *hypothetical* regression line, which is linear and which goes through the origin.

k. How would changes in these items affect the AFN? (1) The dividend payout ratio, (2) the profit margin, (3) the capital intensity ratio, and (4) if NWC begins buying from its suppliers on terms that permit it to pay after 60 days rather than after 30 days. (Consider each item separately and hold all other things constant.)

CHAPTER 4
Financial Planning and Forecasting

- Forecasting sales
- Projecting the assets needed to support sales
- Projecting internally generated funds
- Projecting outside funds needed
- Deciding how to raise funds
- Seeing the effects of a plan on ratios

2001 Balance Sheet
(Millions of $)

Cash & sec.	$ 20	Accts. pay. & accruals	$ 100
Accounts rec.	240	Notes payable	100
Inventories	240	Total CL	$ 200
Total CA	$ 500	L-T debt	100
		Common stock	500
Net fixed assets	500	Retained earnings	200
Total assets	$1,000	Total claims	$1,000

2001 Income Statement
(Millions of $)

Sales		$2,000.00
Less: Var. costs (60%)		1,200.00
Fixed costs		700.00
EBIT		$ 100.00
Interest		16.00
EBT		$ 84.00
Taxes (40%)		33.60
Net income		$ 50.40
Dividends (30%)		$15.12
Add'n to RE		$35.28

Key Ratios

	NWC	Industry	Condition
BEP	10.00%	20.00%	Poor
Profit margin	2.52%	4.00%	"
ROE	7.20%	15.60%	"
DSO	43.80 days	32.00 days	"
Inv. turnover	8.33x	11.00x	"
F. A. turnover	4.00x	5.00x	"
T. A. turnover	2.00x	2.50x	"
Debt/assets	30.00%	36.00%	Good
TIE	6.25x	9.40x	Poor
Current ratio	2.50x	3.00x	"
Payout ratio	30.00%	30.00%	O. K.

Key Assumptions

- Operating at full capacity in 2001.
- Each type of asset grows proportionally with sales.
- Payables and accruals grow proportionally with sales.
- 2001 profit margin (2.52%) and payout (30%) will be maintained.
- Sales are expected to increase by $500 million. (%$\Delta$S = 25%)

Assets

Assets = 0.5 sales

1,250
1,000

Δ Assets=
$(A^*/S_0) \Delta$ Sales
= 0.5(500)
=250.

0   2,000 2,500   **Sales**

$A^*/S_0 = 1,000/2,000 = 0.5 = 1,250/2,500.$

Assets must increase by $250 million. What is the AFN, based on the AFN equation?

$$AFN = (A^*/S_0)\Delta S - (L^*/S_0)\Delta S - M(S_1)(RR)$$
$$= (\$1{,}000/\$2{,}000)(\$500)$$
$$- (\$100/\$2{,}000)(\$500)$$
$$- 0.0252(\$2{,}500)(0.7)$$
$$= \$180.9 \text{ million.}$$

Assumptions about How AFN Will Be Raised

- The payout ratio will remain at 30 percent (d = 30%; RR = 70%).
- No new common stock will be issued.
- Any external funds needed will be raised as debt, 50% notes payable and 50% L-T debt.

2002 Forecasted Income Statement

	2001	Forecast Basis	2002 Forecast
Sales	$2,000	1.25	$2,500
Less: VC	1,200	0.60	1,500
FC	700	0.35	875
EBIT	$ 100		$ 125
Interest	16	→	16
EBT	$ 84		$ 109
Taxes (40%)	34		44
Net income	$ 50		$ 65
Div. (30%)	$15		$19
Add'n to RE	$35		$46

2002 Balance Sheet (Assets)

	2001	Forecast Basis	1st Pass
Cash	$ 20	0.01	$ 25
Accts. rec.	240	0.12	300
Inventories	240	0.12	300
Total CA	$ 500		$ 625
Net FA	500	0.25	625
Total assets	$1,000		$1,250

At full capacity, so all assets must increase in proportion to sales.

2002 Balance Sheet (Claims)

	2001	Forecast Basis	1st Pass
AP/accruals	$ 100	0.05	$ 125
Notes payable	100		100
Total CL	$ 200		$ 225
L-T debt	100		100
Common stk.	500		500
Ret.earnings	200		246
Total claims	$1,000		$1,071

* From income statement.

What is the additional financing needed (AFN)?

- Required increase in assets = $ 250
- Spontaneous increase in liab. = $ 25
- Increase in retained earnings = $ 46
- Total AFN = $ 179

NWC must have the assets to make forecasted sales. The balance sheet must balance. So, we must raise $179 externally.

How will the AFN be financed?

Additional notes payable =
0.5($179) = $89.50

Additional L-T debt =
0.5($179) = $89.50

But this financing will add to interest expense, which will lower NI and retained earnings. We will generally ignore financing feedbacks.

2002 2nd Pass Balance Sheet (Assets)

	1st Pass	AFN	2nd Pass
Cash	$ 25	→	$ 25
Accts. rec.	300	→	300
Inventories	300	→	300
Total CA	$ 625	→	$ 625
Net FA	625	→	625
Total assets	$1,250	→	$1,250

No change in asset requirements.

2002 2nd Pass Balance Sheet (Claims)

	1st Pass	AFN	2nd Pass
AP/accruals	$ 125	→	$ 125
Notes payable	100	+89.5	190
Total CL	$ 225		$ 315
L-T debt	100	+89.5	189
Common stk.	500	→	500
Ret. earnings	246	→	246
Total claims	$1,071		$1,250

Equation AFN = $181 vs. $179. Why different?

- Equation method assumes a constant profit margin, a constant dividend payout, and a constant capital structure.

- Financial statement method is more flexible. More important, it allows different items to grow at different rates.

Ratios

	2001	2002(E)	Industry	
BEP	10.00%	10.00%	20.00%	Poor
Profit margin	2.52%	2.62%	4.00%	"
ROE	7.20%	8.77%	15.60%	"
DSO (days)	43.80	43.80	32.00	"
Inv. turnover	8.33x	8.33x	11.00x	"
F. A. turnover	4.00x	4.00x	5.00x	"
T. A. turnover	2.00x	2.00x	2.50x	"
D/A ratio	30.00%	40.34%	36.00%	"
TIE	6.25x	7.81x	9.4x	"
Current ratio	2.50x	1.99x	3.00x	"
Payout ratio	30.00%	30.00%	30.00%	O. K.

What was the net investment in operating capital?

Oper. cap.$_{2002}$ = NOWC + Net FA
= $625 − $125 + $625
= $1,125.

Oper. cap.$_{2001}$ = $900.

Net inv. in
oper. cap. = $1,125 − $900 = $225.

How much free cash flow was generated in 2002?

FCF = NOPAT – Net inv. in oper. cap.
    = EBIT (1 – T) – Net inv. in oper. cap.
    = $125 (0.6) – $225
    = $75 – $225
    = -$150.

Suppose in 2001 fixed assets had been operated at only 75% of capacity.

$$\text{Capacity Sales} = \frac{\text{Actual sales}}{\text{\% of capacity}}$$

$$= \frac{\$2,000}{0.75} = \$2,667.$$

With the existing fixed assets, sales could be $2,667. Since sales are forecasted at only $2,500, no new fixed assets are needed.

How would the excess capacity situation affect the 2002 AFN?

- The projected increase in fixed assets was $125, the AFN would decrease by $125.

- Since no new fixed assets will be needed, AFN will fall by $125, to

    $179 – $125 = $54.

Q. If sales went up to $3,000, not $2,500, what would the F.A. requirement be?

A. Target ratio = FA/Capacity sales
$$= 500/2,667 = 18.75\%.$$

Have enough F.A. for sales up to $2,667, but need F.A. for another $333 of sales:

$$\Delta FA = 0.1875(333) = \$62.4.$$

How would excess capacity affect the forecasted ratios?

1. Sales wouldn't change but assets would be lower, so turnovers would be better.

2. Less new debt, hence lower interest, so higher profits, EPS, ROE (when financing feedbacks considered).

3. Debt ratio, TIE would improve.

2002 Forecasted Ratios: $S_{02} = \$2,500$

| | % of 2001 Capacity | | |
	100%	75%	Industry
BEP	10.00%	11.11%	20.00%
Profit margin	2.62%	2.62%	4.00%
ROE	8.77%	8.77%	15.60%
DSO (days)	43.80	43.80	32.00
Inv. turnover	8.33x	8.33x	11.00x
F. A. turnover	4.00x	5.00x	5.00x
T. A. turnover	2.00x	2.22x	2.50x
D/A ratio	40.34%	33.71%	36.00%
TIE	7.81x	7.81x	9.40x
Current ratio	1.99x	2.48x	3.00x

How is NWC performing with regard to its receivables and inventories?

- DSO is higher than the industry average, and inventory turnover is lower than the industry average.

- Improvements here would lower current assets, reduce capital requirements, and further improve profitability and other ratios.

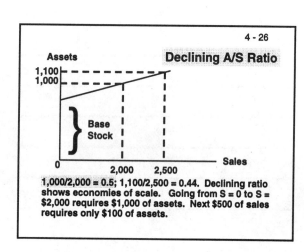

Declining A/S Ratio

1,000/2,000 = 0.5; 1,100/2,500 = 0.44. Declining ratio shows economies of scale. Going from S = 0 to S = $2,000 requires $1,000 of assets. Next $500 of sales requires only $100 of assets.

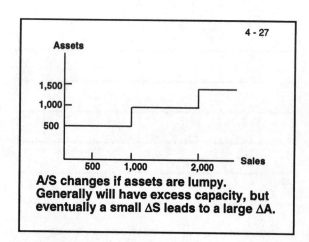

A/S changes if assets are lumpy. Generally will have excess capacity, but eventually a small ΔS leads to a large ΔA.

Regression Analysis for Asset Forecasting

- Get historical data on a good company, then fit a regression line to see how much a given sales increase will require in way of asset increase.

Example of Regression

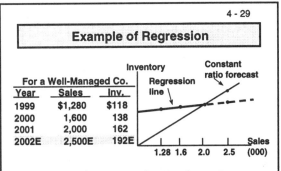

For a Well-Managed Co.		
Year	Sales	Inv.
1999	$1,280	$118
2000	1,600	138
2001	2,000	162
2002E	2,500E	192E

Constant ratio overestimates inventory required to go from $S_1 = 2,000$ to $S_2 = 2,500$.

How would increases in these items affect the AFN?

- Higher dividend payout ratio?
  Increase AFN: Less retained earnings.
- Higher profit margin?
  Decrease AFN: Higher profits, more retained earnings.
- Higher capital intensity ratio, A^*/S_0?
  Increase AFN: Need more assets for given sales increase.
- Pay suppliers in 60 days rather than 30 days?
  Decrease AFN: Trade creditors supply more capital, i.e., L^*/S_0 increases.

Summary: How different factors affect the AFN forecast.

- **Excess capacity:**
  - Existence lowers AFN.
- **Base stocks of assets:**
  - Leads to less-than-proportional asset increases.
- **Economies of scale:**
  - Also leads to less-than-proportional asset increases.
- **Lumpy assets:**
  - Leads to large periodic AFN requirements, recurring excess capacity.

EXAM-TYPE PROBLEMS

4-1. Snowball & Company has the following balance sheet:

Current assets	$ 7,000	A/P & accruals	$ 1,500
Fixed assets	3,000	S-T (3-month) loans	2,000
		Common stock	1,500
		Retained earnings	5,000
Total assets	$10,000	Total claims	$10,000

Snowball's after-tax profit margin is 11 percent, and the company pays out 60 percent of its earnings as dividends. Its sales last year were $10,000; its assets were used to full capacity; no economies of scale exist in the use of assets; and the profit margin and payout ratio are expected to remain constant. The company uses the AFN equation to estimate funds requirements, and it plans to raise any required external capital as short-term bank loans. If sales grow by 50 percent, what will Snowball's current ratio be after it has raised the necessary funds? (1.34)

4-2. Hogan Inc. generated EBIT of $240,000 this past year on $750,000 of sales and using assets of $1,100,000. The interest rate on its existing long-term debt of $640,000 is 12.5 percent and the firm's tax rate is 40 percent. The firm paid a dividend of $1.27 on each of its 37,800 shares outstanding from net income of $96,000. The total book value of equity is $446,364 of which the common stock account equals $335,000. The firm's shares sell for $28.00 per share. The firm forecasts a 10 percent increase in sales, assets, and EBIT next year, and a dividend of $1.40 per share. If the firm needs additional capital funds, it will raise 60 percent with debt and 40 percent with equity. The spontaneous liabilities balance is $13,636. Except for spontaneous liabilities, the firm uses no other sources of current liabilities and will continue this policy in the future. What will be the AFN Hogan will need to balance its projected balance sheet using the projected financial statement method? ($51,156)

4-3. Which of the following statements is most correct?

a. If the capital intensity ratio is high, this permits sales to grow more rapidly without much outside capital.

b. The lower the profit margin, the lower the additional funds needed because less assets are needed to support existing sales.

c. When positive economies of scale are present, linear balance sheet relationships no longer hold. As sales increase, a proportionately greater stock of assets is required to support the higher sales level.

d. Technological considerations often require firms to add fixed assets in large, discrete units. Such assets are called lumpy assets and they affect the firm's financial requirements through the fixed assets-to-sales ratio at different sales levels.

e. The projected financial statement method accounts for changing balance sheet ratios and thus, cyclical changes in the actual sales-to-assets ratio do not have an impact on financing requirements.

5-17 Assume that you recently graduated with a degree in finance and have just reported to work as an investment advisor at the brokerage firm of Smyth Barry & Co. Your first assignment is to explain the nature of the U.S. financial markets to Michelle Varga, a professional tennis player who has just come to the United States from Mexico. Varga is a highly ranked tennis player who expects to invest substantial amounts of money through Smyth Barry. She is also very bright, and, therefore, she would like to understand in general terms what will happen to her money. Your boss has developed the following set of questions that you must ask and answer to explain the U.S. financial system to Varga.

a. What is a market? Differentiate between the following types of markets: physical asset vs. financial markets, spot vs. futures markets, money vs. capital markets, primary vs. secondary markets, and public vs. private markets.

b. What is an initial public offering (IPO) market?

c. If Apple Computer decided to issue additional common stock, and Varga purchased 100 shares of this stock from Merrill Lynch, the underwriter, would this transaction be a primary market transaction or a secondary market transaction? Would it make a difference if Varga purchased previously outstanding Apple stock in the dealer market?

d. Describe the three primary ways in which capital is transferred between savers and borrowers.

e. What are the two leading stock markets? Describe the two basic types of stock markets.

f. What do we call the price that a borrower must pay for debt capital? What is the price of equity capital? What are the four most fundamental factors that affect the cost of money, or the general level of interest rates, in the economy?

g. What is the real risk-free rate of interest (k^*) and the nominal risk-free rate (k_{RF})? How are these two rates measured?

h. Define the terms inflation premium (IP), default risk premium (DRP), liquidity premium (LP), and maturity risk premium (MRP). Which of these premiums is

---

included when determining the interest rate on (1) short-term U.S. Treasury securities, (2) long-term U.S. Treasury securities, (3) short-term corporate securities, and (4) long-term corporate securities? Explain how the premiums would vary over time and among the different securities listed above.

i.   What is the term structure of interest rates? What is a yield curve?

j.   Suppose most investors expect the inflation rate to be 5 percent next year, 6 percent the following year, and 8 percent thereafter. The real risk-free rate is 3 percent. The maturity risk premium is zero for bonds that mature in 1 year or less, 0.1 percent for 2-year bonds, and then the MRP increases by 0.1 percent per year thereafter for 20 years, after which it is stable. What is the interest rate on 1-year, 10-year, and 20-year Treasury bonds? Draw a yield curve with these data. What factors can explain why this constructed yield curve is upward sloping?

k.   At any given time, how would the yield curve facing an AAA-rated company compare with the yield curve for U.S. Treasury securities? At any given time, how would the yield curve facing a BB-rated company compare with the yield curve for U.S. Treasury securities? Draw a graph to illustrate your answer.

l.   What is the pure expectations theory? What does the pure expectations theory imply about the term structure of interest rates?

m.   Suppose that you observe the following term structure for Treasury securities:

Maturity	Yield
1 year	6.0%
2 years	6.2
3 years	6.4
4 years	6.5
5 years	6.5

Assume that the pure expectations theory of the term structure is correct. (This implies that you can use the yield curve given above to "back out" the market's expectations about future interest rates.) What does the market expect will be the interest rate on 1-year securities one year from now? What does the market expect will be the interest rate on 3-year securities two years from now?

n.   Finally, Varga is also interested in investing in countries other than the United States. Describe the various types of risks that arise when investing overseas.

CHAPTER 5
The Financial Environment: Markets, Institutions, and Interest Rates

- Financial markets
- Types of financial institutions
- Determinants of interest rates
- Yield curves

Define These Markets

- Markets in general
- Physical assets vs. Financial assets
- Money vs. Capital
- Primary vs. Secondary
- Spot vs. Futures
- Public vs. Private

What is an Initial Public Offering (IPO) market?

An IPO Market is a subset of the primary market. Firms "go public" by offering shares of their stock to the public for the first time.

Three Primary Ways Capital Is Transferred Between Savers and Borrowers

- Direct transfer
- Investment banking house
- Financial intermediary

The Top 5 Banking Companies in the World, 2000

Bank Name	Country	Total assets
Deutsche Bank AG	Germany	$844 billion
Citigroup	United States	$717 billion
BNP Paribas	France	$702 billion
Bank of Tokyo	Japan	$697 billion
Bank of America	United States	$633 billion

Physical Location Stock Exchanges vs. Electronic Dealer-Based Markets

- Auction market vs. Dealer market (Exchanges vs. OTC)
- NYSE vs. Nasdaq system
- Differences are narrowing

- What do we call the price, or cost, of debt capital?

> **The interest rate**

- What do we call the price, or cost, of equity capital?

> $$\text{Required return} = \text{Dividend yield} + \text{Capital gain}$$

> **What four factors affect the cost of money?**

- **Production opportunities**
- **Time preferences for consumption**
- **Risk**
- **Expected inflation**

> **"Real" Versus "Nominal" Rates**

k^* = Real risk-free rate.
T-bond rate if no inflation;
1% to 4%.

k = Any nominal rate.

k_{RF} = Rate on Treasury securities.

$$k = k^* + IP + DRP + LP + MRP.$$

Here:

k = required rate of return on a debt security.

k^* = real risk-free rate.

IP = inflation premium.

DRP = default risk premium.

LP = liquidity premium.

MRP = maturity risk premium.

Premiums Added to k^* for Different Types of Debt

- S-T Treasury: only IP for S-T inflation
- L-T Treasury: IP for L-T inflation, MRP
- S-T corporate: S-T IP, DRP, LP
- L-T corporate: IP, DRP, MRP, LP

What is the "term structure of interest rates"? What is a "yield curve"?

- Term structure: the relationship between interest rates (or yields) and maturities.
- A graph of the term structure is called the yield curve.

Treasury Yield Curve

Interest Rate (%)

Yield Curve (January 2001)

1 yr	4.8%
5 yr	4.9%
10 yr	5.2%
30 yr	5.6%

Years to Maturity

Yield Curve Construction

Step 1: Find the average expected inflation rate over Years 1 to n:

$$IP_n = \frac{\sum_{t=1}^{n} INFL_t}{n}.$$

Suppose, that inflation is expected to be 5% next year, 6% the following year, and 8% thereafter.

IP_1 = 5%/1.0 = 5.00%.

IP_{10} = [5 + 6 + 8(8)]/10 = 7.50%.

IP_{20} = [5 + 6 + 8(18)]/20 = 7.75%.

Must earn these IPs to break even vs. inflation; these IPs would permit you to earn k* (before taxes).

Step 2: Find MRP Based on This Equation:

$$MRP_t = 0.1\%(t-1).$$

$MRP_1 = 0.1\% \times 0 = 0.0\%.$

$MRP_{10} = 0.1\% \times 9 = 0.9\%.$

$MRP_{20} = 0.1\% \times 19 = 1.9\%.$

Step 3: Add the IPs and MRPs to k*:

$$k_{RF_t} = k^* + IP_t + MRP_t.$$

k_{RF} = Quoted market interest rate on treasury securities.

Assume k* = 3%:

$k_{RF1} = 3.0\% + 5.0\% + 0.0\% = 8.0\%.$

$k_{RF10} = 3.0\% + 7.5\% + 0.9\% = 11.4\%.$

$k_{RF20} = 3.00\% + 7.75\% + 1.90\% = 12.65\%.$

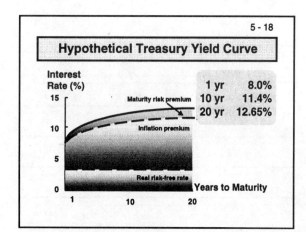

Hypothetical Treasury Yield Curve

1 yr	8.0%
10 yr	11.4%
20 yr	12.65%

What factors can explain the shape of this yield curve?

- This constructed yield curve is upward sloping.

- This is due to increasing expected inflation and an increasing maturity risk premium.

What kind of relationship exists between the Treasury yield curve and the yield curves for corporate issues?

- Corporate yield curves are higher than that of the Treasury bond. However, corporate yield curves are not necessarily parallel to the Treasury curve.

- The spread between a corporate yield curve and the Treasury curve widens as the corporate bond rating decreases.

Hypothetical Treasury and Corporate Yield Curves

How does the volume of corporate bond issues compare to that of Treasury securities?

Gross U.S. Treasury Issuance (in blue)
Investment Grade Corporate Bond Issuance (in red)

Recently, the volume of investment grade corporate bond issues has overtaken Treasury issues.

The Pure Expectations Hypothesis (PEH)

■ Shape of the yield curve depends on investors' expectations about future interest rates.

■ If interest rates are expected to increase, L-T rates will be higher than S-T rates and vice versa. Thus, the yield curve can slope up or down.

■ PEH assumes that MRP = 0.

■ Long-term rates are an average of current and future short-term rates.

■ If PEH is correct, you can use the yield curve to "back out" expected future interest rates.

Observed Treasury Rates

Maturity	Yield
1 year	6.0%
2 years	6.2%
3 years	6.4%
4 years	6.5%
5 years	6.5%

If PEH holds, what does the market expect will be the interest rate on one-year securities, one year from now? Three-year securities, two years from now?

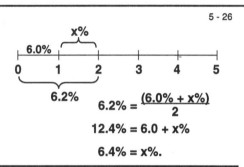

$$6.2\% = \frac{(6.0\% + x\%)}{2}$$

$$12.4\% = 6.0 + x\%$$

$$6.4\% = x\%.$$

PEH tells us that one-year securities will yield 6.4%, one year from now (x%).

$$6.5\% = \frac{[\,2(6.2\%) + 3(x\%)\,]}{5}$$

$$32.5\% = 12.4\% + 3(x\%)$$

$$20.1\% = 3(x\%)$$

$$6.7\% = x\%.$$

PEH tells us that three-year securities will yield 6.7%, two years from now (x%).

Conclusions about PEH

- Some argue that the PEH isn't correct, because securities of different maturities have different risk.
- General view (supported by most evidence) is that lenders prefer S-T securities, and view L-T securities as riskier.
- Thus, investors demand a MRP to get them to hold L-T securities (i.e., MRP > 0).

What various types of risks arise when investing overseas?

Exchange rate risk: If investment is denominated in a currency other than the dollar, the investment's value will depend on what happens to exchange rate.

Country risk: Arises from investing or doing business in a particular country. It depends on the country's economic, political, and social environment.

Two Factors Lead to Exchange Rate Fluctuations

1. Changes in relative inflation will lead to changes in exchange rates.

2. An increase in country risk will also cause that country's currency to fall.

Which countries are the least and most risky?

Safest countries	Riskiest countries
1. Switzerland	141. Sudan
2. Germany	142. Liberia
3. Netherlands	143. Afghanistan
4. Luxembourg	144. Sierra Leone
5. France	145. North Korea
6. United States	

EXAM-TYPE PROBLEMS

5-1. Which of the following statements is most correct?

    a. Since the default risk premium (DRP) and the liquidity premium (LP) are both essentially zero for U.S. Treasury securities, the Treasury yield curve is influenced more heavily by expected inflation than corporate bonds' yield curves, i.e., we can be sure that a given amount of expected inflation will have more effect on the slope of the Treasury yield curve than on the corporate yield curve.

    b. Yield curves for government and corporate bonds can be constructed from data that exist in the marketplace. If the yield curves for several companies were plotted on a graph, along with the yield curve for U.S. Treasury securities, the company with the largest total of DRP plus LP would have the highest yield curve.

    c. An upward-sloping yield curve is the normal situation, because long-term securities have less interest rate risk than shorter-term securities, hence smaller MRPs. Therefore, long-term rates are normally lower than short-term rates.

    d. All of the statements above are true.

    e. All of the above statements are false.

5-2. Assume that the real risk-free rate, k^*, is 4 percent, and inflation is expected to be 9 percent in Year 1, 6 percent in Year 2, and 4 percent thereafter. Assume also that all Treasury bonds are highly liquid and free of default risk. If 2-year and 5-year Treasury bonds both yield 12 percent, what is the difference in the maturity risk premiums (MRPs) on the two bonds, i.e., what is $MRP_5 - MRP_2$? (+2.1%)

5-3. A Treasury bond that matures in 8 years has a yield of 6.6 percent. An 8-year corporate bond has a yield of 9.3 percent. Assume that the liquidity premium on the corporate bond is 0.6 percent. What is the default risk premium on the corporate bond? (2.1%)

6-21   Assume that you recently graduated with a major in finance, and you just landed a job as a financial planner with Merrill Finch Inc., a large financial services corporation. Your first assignment is to invest $100,000 for a client. Because the funds are to be invested in a business at the end of 1 year, you have been instructed to plan for a 1-year holding period. Further, your boss has restricted you to the following investment alternatives, shown with their probabilities and associated outcomes. (Disregard for now the items at the bottom of the data; you will fill in the blanks later.)

| | | Returns on Alternative Investments | | | | | |
| | | Estimated Rate of Return | | | | | |
State of the Economy	Prob.	T-Bills	High Tech	Collec-tions	U.S. Rubber	Market Portfolio	2-stock Portfolio
Recession	0.1	8.0%	-22.0%	28.0%	10.0%*	-13.0%	3.0%
Below avg	0.2	8.0	-2.0	14.7	-10.0	1.0	
Average	0.4	8.0	20.0	0.0	7.0	15.0	10.0%
Above avg	0.2	8.0	35.0	-10.0	45.0	29.0	
Boom	0.1	8.0	50.0	-20.0	30.0	43.0	15.0
$\hat{k}$				1.7%	13.8%	15.0%	
σ		0.0		13.4	18.8	15.3	3.3
CV				7.9	1.4	1.0	0.3
b				-0.87	0.89		

* Note that the estimated returns of U.S. Rubber do not always move in the same direction as the overall economy. For example, when the economy is below average, consumers purchase fewer tires than they would if the economy was stronger. However, if the economy is in a flat-out recession, a large number of consumers who were planning to purchase a new car may choose to wait and instead purchase new tires for the car they currently own. Under these circumstances, we would expect U.S. Rubber's stock price to be higher if there is a recession than if the economy was just below average.

Merrill Finch's economic forecasting staff has developed probability estimates for the state of the economy, and its security analysts have developed a sophisticated computer program, which was used to estimate the rate of return on each alternative under each state of the economy. High Tech Inc. is an electronics firm; Collections Inc. collects past-due debts; and U.S. Rubber manufactures tires and various other rubber and plastics products. Merrill Finch also maintains a "market portfolio" that owns a market-weighted fraction of all publicly traded stocks; you can invest in that portfolio, and thus obtain average stock market results. Given the situation as described, answer the following questions.

a.   (1) Why is the T-bill's return independent of the state of the economy? Do T-bills promise a completely risk-free return?

(2) Why are High Tech's returns expected to move with the economy whereas Collections' are expected to move counter to the economy?

b. Calculate the expected rate of return on each alternative and fill in the blanks on the row for $\hat{k}$ in the table above.

c. You should recognize that basing a decision solely on expected returns is only appropriate for risk-neutral individuals. Since your client, like virtually everyone, is risk averse, the riskiness of each alternative is an important aspect of the decision. One possible measure of risk is the standard deviation of returns.

(1) Calculate this value for each alternative, and fill in the blank on the row for σ in the table above.

(2) What type of risk is measured by the standard deviation?

(3) Draw a graph that shows *roughly* the shape of the probability distributions for High Tech, U.S. Rubber, and T-bills.

d. Suppose you suddenly remembered that the *coefficient of variation (CV)* is generally regarded as being a better measure of stand-alone risk than the standard deviation when the alternatives being considered have widely differing expected returns. Calculate the missing CVs, and fill in the blanks on the row for CV in the table above. Does the CV produce the same risk rankings as the standard deviation?

e. Suppose you created a 2-stock portfolio by investing $50,000 in High Tech and $50,000 in Collections.

(1) Calculate the expected return ($\hat{k}_p$), the standard deviation (σ_p), and the coefficient of variation (CV_p) for this portfolio and fill in the appropriate blanks in the table above.

(2) How does the riskiness of this 2-stock portfolio compare with the riskiness of the individual stocks if they were held in isolation?

f. Suppose an investor starts with a portfolio consisting of one randomly selected stock. What would happen (1) to the riskiness and (2) to the expected return of the portfolio as more and more randomly selected stocks were added to the portfolio? What is the implication for investors? Draw a graph of the two portfolios to illustrate your answer.

g. (1) Should portfolio effects impact the way investors think about the riskiness of individual stocks?

(2) If you decided to hold a 1-stock portfolio, and consequently were exposed to more risk than diversified investors, could you expect to be compensated for

all of your risk; that is, could you earn a risk premium on that part of your risk that you could have eliminated by diversifying?

h. The expected rates of return and the beta coefficients of the alternatives as supplied by Merrill Finch's computer program are as follows:

Security	Return ($\hat{k}$)	Risk (Beta)
High Tech	17.4%	1.30
Market	15.0	1.00
U.S. Rubber	13.8	0.89
T-bills	8.0	0.00
Collections	1.7	-0.87

(1) What is a beta coefficient, and how are betas used in risk analysis?

(2) Do the expected returns appear to be related to each alternative's market risk?

(3) Is it possible to choose among the alternatives on the basis of the information developed thus far? Use the data given at the start of the problem to construct a graph that shows how the T-bill's, High Tech's, and Collections' beta coefficients are calculated. Then discuss what betas measure and how they are used in risk analysis.

i. The yield curve is currently flat, that is, long-term Treasury bonds also have an 8 percent yield. Consequently, Merrill Finch assumes that the risk-free rate is 8 percent.

(1) Write out the Security Market Line (SML) equation, use it to calculate the required rate of return on each alternative, and then graph the relationship between the expected and required rates of return.

(2) How do the expected rates of return compare with the required rates of return?

(3) Does the fact that Collections has an expected return that is less than the T-bill rate make any sense?

(4) What would be the market risk and the required return of a 50-50 portfolio of High Tech and Collections? Of High Tech and U.S. Rubber?

j. (1) Suppose investors raised their inflation expectations by 3 percentage points over current estimates as reflected in the 8 percent risk-free rate. What effect would higher inflation have on the SML and on the returns required on high- and low-risk securities?

(2) Suppose instead that investors' risk aversion increased enough to cause the market risk premium to increase by 3 percentage points. (Inflation remains constant.) What effect would this have on the SML and on returns of high- and low-risk securities?

CHAPTER 6
Risk and Rates of Return

- Stand-alone risk
- Portfolio risk
- Risk & return: CAPM/SML

What is investment risk?

Investment risk pertains to the probability of actually earning a low or negative return.

The greater the chance of low or negative returns, the riskier the investment.

Probability distribution

Firm X

Firm Y

Rate of Return (%)

-70   0   15   100

Expected Rate of Return

Selected Realized Returns, 1926-1999

	Average Return	Standard Deviation
Small-company stocks	17.6%	33.6%
Large-company stocks	13.3	20.1
Long-term corporate bonds	5.9	8.7
Long-term government bonds	5.5	9.3
U.S. Treasury bills	3.8	3.2

Source: Based on *Stocks, Bonds, Bills, and Inflation: (Valuation Edition) 2000 Yearbook* (Chicago: Ibbotson Associates, 2000)

Investment Alternatives
(Given in the problem)

Economy	Prob.	T-Bill	HT	Coll	USR	MP
Recession	0.1	8.0%	-22.0%	28.0%	10.0%	-13.0%
Below avg.	0.2	8.0	-2.0	14.7	-10.0	1.0
Average	0.4	8.0	20.0	0.0	7.0	15.0
Above avg.	0.2	8.0	35.0	-10.0	45.0	29.0
Boom	0.1	8.0	50.0	-20.0	30.0	43.0
	1.0					

Why is the T-bill return independent of the economy?

Will return the promised 8% regardless of the economy.

Do T-bills promise a completely risk-free return?

No, T-bills are still exposed to the risk of inflation.

However, not much unexpected inflation is likely to occur over a relatively short period.

Do the returns of HT and Coll. move with or counter to the economy?

- HT: Moves with the economy, and has a positive correlation. This is typical.
- Coll: Is countercyclical of the economy, and has a negative correlation. This is unusual.

Calculate the expected rate of return on each alternative:

$\hat{k}$ = expected rate of return.

$$\hat{k} = \sum_{i=1}^{n} k_i P_i.$$

$\hat{k}_{HT}$ = (-22%)0.1 + (-2%)0.20
+ (20%)0.40 + (35%)0.20
+ (50%)0.1 = 17.4%.

	$\hat{k}$
HT	17.4%
Market	15.0
USR	13.8
T-bill	8.0
Coll.	1.7

HT appears to be the best, but is it really?

What's the standard deviation of returns for each alternative?

σ = Standard deviation.

$$\sigma = \sqrt{\text{Variance}} = \sqrt{\sigma^2}$$

$$\sigma = \sqrt{\sum_{i=1}^{n}(k_i - \hat{k})^2 P_i}.$$

$$\sigma = \sqrt{\sum_{i=1}^{n}(k_i - \hat{k})^2 P_i}.$$

$$\sigma_{\text{T-bills}} = \left[\begin{array}{l} (8.0 - 8.0)^2 0.1 + (8.0 - 8.0)^2 0.2 \\ + (8.0 - 8.0)^2 0.4 + (8.0 - 8.0)^2 0.2 \\ + (8.0 - 8.0)^2 0.1 \end{array}\right]^{1/2}$$

$\sigma_{\text{T-bills}} = $ 0.0%. $\quad \sigma_{\text{Coll}} = $ 13.4%.
$\sigma_{\text{HT}} = $ 20.0%. $\quad \sigma_{\text{USR}} = $ 18.8%.
$\quad\quad\quad\quad\quad\quad \sigma_{\text{M}} = $ 15.3%.

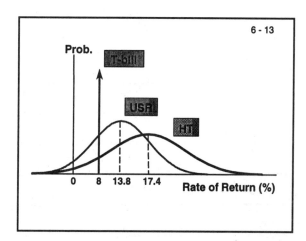

- Standard deviation (σ_I) measures total, or stand-alone, risk.

- The larger the σ_I, the lower the probability that actual returns will be close to the expected return.

Expected Returns vs. Risk

Security	Expected Return	Risk, σ
HT	17.4%	20.0%
Market	15.0	15.3
USR	13.8*	18.8*
T-bills	8.0	0.0
Coll.	1.7*	13.4*

*Seems misplaced.

Coefficient of Variation (CV)

Standardized measure of dispersion about the expected value:

$$CV = \frac{\text{Std dev}}{\text{Mean}} = \frac{\sigma}{\hat{k}}.$$

Shows risk per unit of return.

---

6 - 17

Prob.

A → ← B

0   Rate of Return (%)

$\sigma_A = \sigma_B$, but A is riskier because larger probability of losses.

$$\frac{\sigma}{\hat{k}} = CV_A > CV_B.$$

---

6 - 18

Portfolio Risk and Return

Assume a two-stock portfolio with $50,000 in HT and $50,000 in Collections.

Calculate $\hat{k}_p$ and σ_p.

Portfolio Return, $\hat{k}_p$

$\hat{k}_p$ is a weighted average:

$$\hat{k}_p = \sum_{i=1}^{n} w_i \hat{k}_i.$$

$\hat{k}_p = 0.5(17.4\%) + 0.5(1.7\%) = 9.6\%.$

$\hat{k}_p$ is between $\hat{k}_{HT}$ and $\hat{k}_{COLL}$.

Alternative Method

		Estimated Return		
Economy	Prob.	HT	Coll.	Port.
Recession	0.10	-22.0%	28.0%	3.0%
Below avg.	0.20	-2.0	14.7	6.4
Average	0.40	20.0	0.0	10.0
Above avg.	0.20	35.0	-10.0	12.5
Boom	0.10	50.0	-20.0	15.0

$\hat{k}_p = (3.0\%)0.10 + (6.4\%)0.20 + (10.0\%)0.40$
$+ (12.5\%)0.20 + (15.0\%)0.10 = 9.6\%.$

$$\sigma_p = \left[\begin{array}{l} (3.0 - 9.6)^2 0.10 \\ + (6.4 - 9.6)^2 0.20 \\ + (10.0 - 9.6)^2 0.40 \\ + (12.5 - 9.6)^2 0.20 \\ + (15.0 - 9.6)^2 0.10 \end{array} \right]^{1/2} = 3.3\%.$$

$$CV_p = \frac{3.3\%}{9.6\%} = 0.34.$$

- $\sigma_p = 3.3\%$ is much lower than that of either stock (20% and 13.4%).

- $\sigma_p = 3.3\%$ is lower than average of HT and Coll = 16.7%.

- $\therefore$ Portfolio provides average $\hat{k}$ but lower risk.

- Reason: negative correlation.

General statements about risk

- Most stocks are positively correlated. $r_{k,m} \approx 0.65$.

- $\sigma \approx 35\%$ for an average stock.

- Combining stocks generally lowers risk.

Returns Distributions for Two Perfectly Negatively Correlated Stocks (r = -1.0) and for Portfolio WM

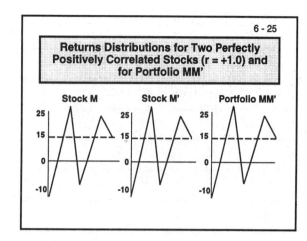

Returns Distributions for Two Perfectly Positively Correlated Stocks (r = +1.0) and for Portfolio MM'

Stock M   Stock M'   Portfolio MM'

---

6 - 26

What would happen to the riskiness of an average 1-stock portfolio as more randomly selected stocks were added?

■ σ_p would decrease because the added stocks would not be perfectly correlated but $\hat{k}_p$ would remain relatively constant.

Even with large N, $\sigma_p \approx 20\%$

σ_p (%)

Company-Specific Risk

Stand-Alone Risk, σ_p

Market Risk

Stocks in Portfolio

- As more stocks are added, each new stock has a smaller risk-reducing impact.

- σ_p falls very slowly after about 10 stocks are included, and after 40 stocks, there is little, if any, effect. The lower limit for σ_p is about 20% = σ_M .

Stand-alone risk	=	Market risk	+	Firm-specific risk

Market risk is that part of a security's stand-alone risk that *cannot* be eliminated by diversification, and it is measured by beta.

Firm-specific risk is that part of a security's stand-alone risk that can be eliminated by proper diversification.

■ By forming portfolios, we can eliminate about half the riskiness of individual stocks (35% vs. 20%).

If you chose to hold a one-stock portfolio and thus are exposed to more risk than diversified investors, would you be compensated for all the risk you bear?

■ NO!

■ Stand-alone risk as measured by a stock's σ or CV is not important to a well-diversified investor.

■ Rational, risk-averse investors are concerned with σ_p, which is based on market risk.

■ There can only be one price, hence market return, for a given security. Therefore, no compensation can be earned for the additional risk of a one-stock portfolio.

■ Beta measures a stock's market risk. It shows a stock's volatility relative to the market.

■ Beta shows how risky a stock is if the stock is held in a well-diversified portfolio.

How are betas calculated?

■ Run a regression of past returns on Stock *i* versus returns on the market. Returns = D/P + g.

■ The slope of the regression line is defined as the beta coefficient.

Illustration of Beta Calculation:

Regression line:
$$\hat{k}_I = -2.59 + 1.44 \, \hat{k}_M$$

Year	$\bar{k}_M$	$\bar{k}_I$
1	15%	18%
2	-5	-10
3	12	16

- If beta = 1.0, average stock.

- If beta > 1.0, stock riskier than average.

- If beta < 1.0, stock less risky than average.

- Most stocks have betas in the range of 0.5 to 1.5.

List of Beta Coefficients

Stock	Beta
Merrill Lynch	1.85
America Online	1.60
General Electric	1.25
Microsoft Corp.	1.00
Coca-Cola	1.00
IBM	1.00
Procter & Gamble	0.85
Energen Corp.	0.80
Heinz	0.70
Empire District Electric	0.45

Can a beta be negative?

Yes, if $r_{I,m}$ is negative. Then in a "beta graph" the regression line will slope downward. Though, a negative beta is highly unlikely.

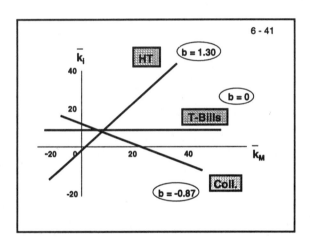

Security	Expected Return	Risk (Beta)
HT	17.4%	1.30
Market	15.0	1.00
USR	13.8	0.89
T-bills	8.0	0.00
Coll.	1.7	-0.87

Riskier securities have higher returns, so the rank order is OK.

Use the SML to calculate the required returns.

SML: $k_i = k_{RF} + (k_M - k_{RF})b_i$.

- Assume k_{RF} = 8%.
- Note that $k_M = \hat{k}_M$ is 15%. (Equil.)
- $RP_M = k_M - k_{RF} = 15\% - 8\% = 7\%$.

Required Rates of Return

$$k_{HT} = 8.0\% + (15.0\% - 8.0\%)(1.30)$$
$$= 8.0\% + (7\%)(1.30)$$
$$= 8.0\% + 9.1\% \qquad = 17.10\%.$$
$$k_M = 8.0\% + (7\%)(1.00) \qquad = 15.00\%.$$
$$k_{USR} = 8.0\% + (7\%)(0.89) \qquad = 14.23\%.$$
$$k_{T\text{-bill}} = 8.0\% + (7\%)(0.00) \qquad = 8.00\%.$$
$$k_{Coll} = 8.0\% + (7\%)(-0.87) \qquad = 1.91\%.$$

Expected vs. Required Returns

	$\hat{k}$	k	
HT	17.4%	17.1%	Undervalued: $\hat{k} > k$
Market	15.0	15.0	Fairly valued
USR	13.8	14.2	Overvalued: $\hat{k} < k$
T-bills	8.0	8.0	Fairly valued
Coll.	1.7	1.9	Overvalued: $\hat{k} < k$

SML: $k_I = 8\% + (15\% - 8\%) b_I$.

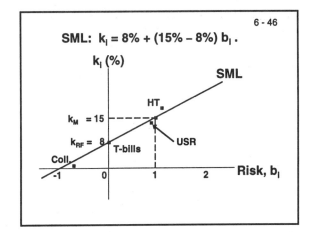

Calculate beta for a portfolio with 50% HT and 50% Collections

b_p = Weighted average
= $0.5(b_{HT}) + 0.5(b_{Coll})$
= $0.5(1.30) + 0.5(-0.87)$
= 0.215.

The required return on the HT/Coll. portfolio is:

k_p = Weighted average k
= $0.5(17.1\%) + 0.5(1.9\%) = 9.5\%$.

Or use SML:

$k_p = k_{RF} + (k_M - k_{RF}) b_p$
= $8.0\% + (15.0\% - 8.0\%)(0.215)$
= $8.0\% + 7\%(0.215) = 9.5\%$.

If investors raise inflation expectations by 3%, what would happen to the SML?

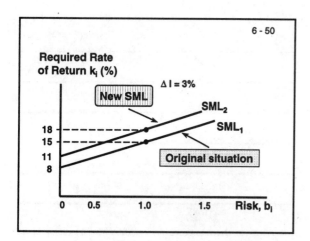

Required Rate of Return k_i (%)

New SML $\Delta I = 3\%$

SML$_2$

SML$_1$

18
15
11
8

Original situation

0   0.5   1.0   1.5   Risk, b_i

If inflation did not change but risk aversion increased enough to cause the market risk premium to increase by 3 percentage points, what would happen to the SML?

---

6 - 52

Required Rate of Return (%)

After increase in risk aversion

$k_{M_2} = 18\%$

$k_{M_1} = 15\%$

SML$_2$

SML$_1$

18

15

8

$\Delta RP_M = 3\%$

Original situation

Risk, b$_i$

1.0

---

6 - 53

Has the CAPM been verified through empirical tests?

■ Not completely. Those statistical tests have problems that make verification almost impossible.

---

6 - 54

■ Investors seem to be concerned with both market risk and total risk. Therefore, the SML may not produce a correct estimate of k$_i$:

$$k_i = k_{RF} + (k_M - k_{RF})b_i + ?$$

6 - 55

■ Also, CAPM/SML concepts are
based on expectations, yet betas
are calculated using historical data.
A company's historical data may
not reflect investors' expectations
about future riskiness.

_____

_____

_____

_____

_____

_____

_____

EXAM-TYPE PROBLEMS

6-1. For markets to be in equilibrium (that is, for there to be no strong pressure for prices to depart from their current levels),

   a. The expected rate of return must be equal to the required rate of return; that is, $\hat{k} = k$.

   b. The past realized rate of return must be equal to the expected rate of return; that is, $\bar{k} = \hat{k}$.

   c. The required rate of return must equal the realized rate of return; that is, $k = \bar{k}$.

   d. All three of the above statements must hold for equilibrium to exist; that is, $\hat{k} = k = \bar{k}$.

   e. None of the above statements is correct.

6-2. Which of the following statements is most correct?

   a. According to CAPM theory, the required rate of return on a given stock can be found by use of the SML equation:

$$k_i = k_{RF} + (k_M - k_{RF})b_i.$$

   Expectations for inflation are not reflected anywhere in this equation, even indirectly, and because of that the text notes that the CAPM may not be strictly correct.

   b. If the required rate of return is given by the SML equation as set forth in answer a, there is nothing a financial manager can do to change his or her company's cost of capital, because each of the elements in the equation is determined exclusively by the market, not by the type of actions a company's management can take, even in the long run.

   c. Assume that the required rate of return on the market is currently $k_M = 15\%$, and that k_M remains fixed at that level. If the yield curve has a steep upward slope, the calculated market risk premium would be larger if the 30-day T-bill rate were used as the risk-free rate than if the 30-year T-bond rate were used as k_{RF}.

   d. Statements a and b are true.

   e. Statements a and c are true.

6-3. You hold a diversified portfolio consisting of a $5,000 investment in each of 20 different common stocks. The portfolio beta is equal to 1.15. You have decided to sell one of your stocks, a lead mining stock whose b = 1.0, for $5,000 net and to use the proceeds to buy $5,000 of stock in a steel company whose b = 2.0. What will be the portfolio's new beta? (1.20)

6-4. Electro Inc. has a beta of 1.7, Flowers Galore has a beta of 0.6, the expected rate of return on an average stock is 14 percent, and the risk-free rate of return is 7.8 percent. By how much does the required return on the riskier stock exceed the required return on the less risky stock? (+6.82%)

7-51 Assume that you are nearing graduation and that you have applied for a job with a local bank, First National Bank. As part of the bank's evaluation process, you have been asked to take an examination that covers several financial analysis techniques. The first section of the test addresses time value of money analysis. See how you would do by answering the following questions.

a. Draw time lines for (1) a $100 lump sum cash flow at the end of Year 2, (2) an ordinary annuity of $100 per year for 3 years, and (3) an uneven cash flow stream of -$50, $100, $75, and $50 at the end of Years 0 through 3.

b. (1) What is the future value of an initial $100 after 3 years if it is invested in an account paying 10 percent, annual compounding?

   (2) What is the present value of $100 to be received in 3 years if the appropriate interest rate is 10 percent, annual compounding?

c. We sometimes need to find how long it will take a sum of money (or anything else) to grow to some specified amount. For example, if a company's sales are growing at a rate of 20 percent per year, how long will it take sales to double?

d. What is the difference between an ordinary annuity and an annuity due? What type of annuity is shown below? How would you change it to the other type of annuity?

e. (1) What is the future value of a 3-year ordinary annuity of $100 if the appropriate interest rate is 10 percent, annual compounding?

   (2) What is the present value of the annuity?

   (3) What would the future and present values be if the annuity were an annuity due?

f. What is the present value of the following uneven cash flow stream? The appropriate interest rate is 10 percent, compounded annually.

g. What annual interest rate will cause $100 to grow to $125.97 in 3 years?

h. (1) Will the future value be larger or smaller if we compound an initial amount more often than annually, for example, every 6 months, or *semiannually*, holding the stated interest rate constant? Why?

(2) Define (a) the stated, or quoted, or nominal, rate, (b) the periodic rate, and (c) the effective annual rate (EAR).

(3) What is the effective annual rate corresponding to a nominal rate of 10 percent, compounded semiannually? Compounded quarterly? Compounded daily?

(4) What is the future value of $100 after 3 years under 10 percent semiannual compounding? Quarterly compounding?

i. When will the effective annual rate be equal to the nominal (quoted) rate?

j. (1) What is the value at the end of Year 3 of the following cash flow stream if the quoted interest rate is 10 percent, compounded semiannually?

(2) What is the PV of the same stream?

(3) Is the stream an annuity?

(4) An important rule is that you should *never* show a nominal rate on a time line or use it in calculations unless what condition holds? (Hint: Think of annual compounding, when $i_{Nom} = EAR = i_{PER}$.) What would be wrong with your answer to parts j(1) and j(2) if you used the nominal rate, 10 percent, rather than the periodic rate, $i_{Nom}/2 = 10\%/2 = 5\%$?

k. (1) Construct an amortization schedule for a $1,000, 10 percent, annual compounding loan with 3 equal installments.

(2) What is the annual interest expense for the borrower, and the annual interest income for the lender, during Year 2?

Parts l through o require a financial calculator.

l. Suppose on January 1, 2002, you deposit $100 in an account that pays a nominal, or quoted, interest rate of 10 percent, with interest added (compounded) 365 times per year. How much would you have in your account on October 1, or after 9 months (273 days)?

m. Now, suppose you left your money in the bank for 21 months. Thus, on January 1, 2002, you deposit $100 in an account that pays 10 percent, daily compounding, with a 365-day year. How much would be in your account on October 1, 2003, or 273 + 365 = 638 days later?

n. Suppose someone offered to sell you a note calling for the payment of $1,000 15 months from today (455 days). She offers to sell it to you for $850. You have $850 in a bank time deposit that pays a 7 percent nominal rate with daily (365 days per year) compounding, and you plan to leave the money in the bank unless you buy the note. The note is not risky—you are sure it will be paid on schedule. Should you buy the note? Check the decision in three ways: (1) by comparing your future value if you buy the note versus leaving your money in the bank, (2) by comparing the PV of the note with your current bank account, and (3) by comparing the EAR on the note versus that of the bank account.

o. Suppose the note discussed in part n had a cost of $850, but called for 5 quarterly payments of $190 each, with the first payment due in 3 months rather than $1,000 at the end of 15 months. Would it be a good investment for you? (Assume that today is January 1, 2002, and that the first payment will be due April 1, 2002.)

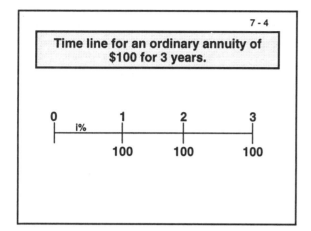

Time line for an ordinary annuity of $100 for 3 years.

7 - 4

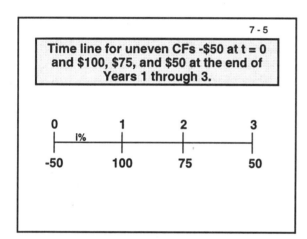

Time line for uneven CFs -$50 at t = 0 and $100, $75, and $50 at the end of Years 1 through 3.

7 - 5

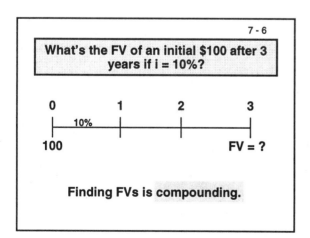

What's the FV of an initial $100 after 3 years if i = 10%?

7 - 6

Finding FVs is compounding.

After 1 year:

$$FV_1 = PV + INT_1 = PV + PV(i)$$
$$= PV(1 + i)$$
$$= \$100(1.10)$$
$$= \$110.00.$$

After 2 years:

$$FV_2 = PV(1 + i)^2$$
$$= \$100(1.10)^2$$
$$= \$121.00.$$

After 3 years:

$$FV_3 = PV(1 + i)^3$$
$$= \$100(1.10)^3$$
$$= \$133.10.$$

In general,

$$FV_n = PV(1 + i)^n.$$

Four Ways to Find FVs

- Solve the equation with a regular calculator.
- Use tables.
- Use a financial calculator.
- Use a spreadsheet.

Financial Calculator Solution

Financial calculators solve this equation:

$$FV_n = PV(1 + i)^n.$$

There are 4 variables. If 3 are known, the calculator will solve for the 4th.

Here's the setup to find FV:

```
INPUTS   3     10    -100    0
        [N]  [I/YR]  [PV]  [PMT]  [FV]
OUTPUT                            133.10
```

Clearing automatically sets everything to 0, but for safety enter PMT = 0.

Set: P/YR = 1, END

What's the PV of $100 due in 3 years if i = 10%?

Finding PVs is <u>discounting</u>, and it's the reverse of compounding.

PV = ?

Solve $FV_n = PV(1 + i)^n$ for PV:

$$PV = \frac{FV_n}{(1 + i)^n} = FV_n\left(\frac{1}{1 + i}\right)^n.$$

$$PV = \$100\left(\frac{1}{1.10}\right)^3 = \$100(PVIF_{i,n})$$

$$= \$100(0.7513) = \$75.13.$$

Financial Calculator Solution

INPUTS	3	10		0	100
	N	I/YR	PV	PMT	FV
OUTPUT			-75.13		

Either PV or FV must be negative. Here PV = -75.13. Put in \$75.13 today, take out 100 after 3 years.

If sales grow at 20% per year, how long before sales double?

Solve for n:

$$FV_n = \$1(1 + i)^n;$$
$$\$2 = \$1(1.20)^n$$

Use calculator to solve, see next slide.

INPUTS

N	20 I/YR	-1 PV	0 PMT	2 FV

OUTPUT 3.8

Graphical Illustration:

What's the difference between an ordinary annuity and an annuity due?

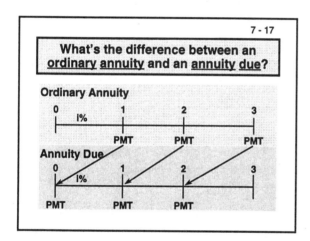

Ordinary Annuity

Annuity Due

What's the FV of a 3-year ordinary annuity of $100 at 10%?

FV = 331

Financial Calculator Solution

INPUTS	3	10	0	-100	
	N	I/YR	PV	PMT	FV
OUTPUT					331.00

Have payments but no lump sum PV, so enter 0 for present value.

What's the PV of this ordinary annuity?

$$90.91$$
$$82.64$$
$$\underline{75.13}$$
$$\underline{248.68} = PV$$

INPUTS	3	10		100	0
	N	I/YR	PV	PMT	FV
OUTPUT			-248.69		

Have payments but no lump sum FV, so enter 0 for future value.

Find the FV and PV if the annuity were an annuity due.

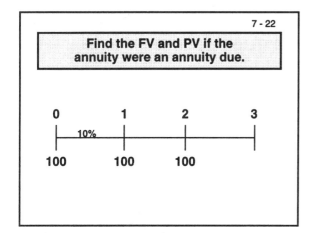

```
0        1        2        3
|--------|--------|--------|
   10%
100      100      100
```

Switch from "End" to "Begin."
Then enter variables to find
PVA$_3$ = \$273.55.

```
INPUTS     3     10          100    0
          [ N ] [I/YR] [PV] [PMT] [FV]
OUTPUT                -273.55
```

Then enter PV = 0 and press FV to find
FV = \$364.10.

What is the PV of this uneven cash flow stream?

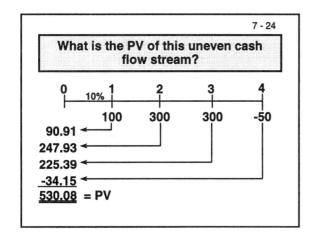

```
0       1        2        3        4
|-------|--------|--------|--------|
   10%
       100      300      300      -50
90.91 ◄─┘
247.93 ◄─────────┘
225.39 ◄──────────────────┘
-34.15 ◄───────────────────────────┘
530.08  = PV
```

■ Input in "CFLO" register:

$CF_0 = 0$

$CF_1 = 100$

$CF_2 = 300$

$CF_3 = 300$

$CF_4 = -50$

■ Enter I = 10, then press NPV button to get NPV = $530.09. (Here NPV = PV.)

What interest rate would cause $100 to grow to $125.97 in 3 years?

$$\$100 (1 + i)^3 = \$125.97.$$

INPUTS	3		-100	0	125.97
	N	I/YR	PV	PMT	FV
OUTPUT		8%			

The Power of Compound Interest

A 20-year old student wants to start saving for retirement. She plans to save $3 a day. Every day, she puts $3 in her drawer. At the end of the year, she invests the accumulated savings ($1,095) in an online stock account. The stock account has an expected annual return of 12%.

How much money by the age of 65?

INPUTS	45	12	0	-1095	
	N	I/YR	PV	PMT	FV
OUTPUT				1,487,261.89	

If she begins saving today, and sticks to her plan, she will have $1,487,261.89 by the age of 65.

How much would a 40-year old investor accumulate by this method?

INPUTS	25	12	0	-1095	
	N	I/YR	PV	PMT	FV
OUTPUT				146,000.59	

Waiting until 40, the investor will only have $146,000.59, which is over $1.3 million less than if saving began at 20. So it pays to get started early.

How much would the 40-year old investor need to save to accumulate as much as the 20-year old?

INPUTS	25	12	0	1487261.89	
	N	I/YR	PV	PMT	FV
OUTPUT			-11,154.42		

The 40-year old investor would have to save $11,154.42 every year, or $30.56 per day to have as much as the investor beginning at the age of 20.

Will the FV of a lump sum be larger or smaller if we compound more often, holding the stated I% constant? Why?

LARGER! If compounding is more frequent than once a year--for example, semiannually, quarterly, or daily--interest is earned on interest more often.

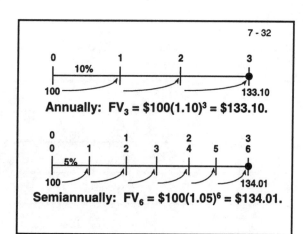

Annually: $FV_3 = \$100(1.10)^3 = \$133.10$.

Semiannually: $FV_6 = \$100(1.05)^6 = \$134.01$.

We will deal with 3 different rates:

i_{Nom} = nominal, or stated, or quoted, rate per year.

i_{Per} = periodic rate.

EAR = EFF% = effective annual rate .

- i_{Nom} is stated in contracts. Periods per year (m) must also be given.
- Examples:
  - 8%; Quarterly
  - 8%, Daily interest (365 days)

- Periodic rate = i_{Per} = i_{Nom}/m, where m is number of compounding periods per year. m = 4 for quarterly, 12 for monthly, and 360 or 365 for daily compounding.
- Examples:

  8% quarterly: i_{Per} = 8%/4 = 2%.

  8% daily (365): i_{Per} = 8%/365 = 0.021918%.

- Effective Annual Rate (EAR = EFF%):
  The annual rate that causes PV to grow to the same FV as under multi-period compounding.
  Example: EFF% for 10%, semiannual:
  $$FV = (1 + i_{Nom}/m)^m$$
  $$= (1.05)^2 = 1.1025.$$
  EFF% = 10.25% because
  $$(1.1025)^1 = 1.1025.$$
  Any PV would grow to same FV at 10.25% annually or 10% semiannually.

■ An investment with monthly payments is different from one with quarterly payments. Must put on EFF% basis to compare rates of return. Use EFF% only for comparisons.

■ Banks say "interest paid daily." Same as compounded daily.

How do we find EFF% for a nominal rate of 10%, compounded semiannually?

$$EFF = \left(1 + \frac{i_{Nom}}{m}\right)^m - 1$$

$$= \left(1 + \frac{0.10}{2}\right)^2 - 1.0$$

$$= (1.05)^2 - 1.0$$

$$= 0.1025 = 10.25\%.$$

Or use a financial calculator.

EAR = EFF% of 10%

EAR_{Annual} = 10%.

EAR_Q = $(1 + 0.10/4)^4 - 1$ = 10.38%.

EAR_M = $(1 + 0.10/12)^{12} - 1$ = 10.47%.

$EAR_{D(365)}$ = $(1 + 0.10/365)^{365} - 1$ = 10.52%.

Can the effective rate ever be equal to the nominal rate?

■ **Yes, but only if annual compounding is used, i.e., if m = 1.**

■ **If m > 1, EFF% will always be greater than the nominal rate.**

When is each rate used?

i_{Nom}: **Written into contracts, quoted by banks and brokers. <u>Not</u> used in calculations or shown on time lines.**

i_{Per}: **Used in calculations, shown on time lines.**

If i_{Nom} has annual compounding, then $i_{Per} = i_{Nom}/1 = i_{Nom}$.

EAR = EFF%: Used to compare returns on investments with different payments per year.

(Used for calculations if and only if dealing with annuities where payments don't match interest compounding periods.)

FV of $100 after 3 years under 10% semiannual compounding? Quarterly?

$$FV_n = PV\left(1 + \frac{i_{Nom}}{m}\right)^{mn}.$$

$$FV_{3S} = \$100\left(1 + \frac{0.10}{2}\right)^{2\times3}$$

$$= \$100(1.05)^6 = \$134.01.$$

$$FV_{3Q} = \$100(1.025)^{12} = \$134.49.$$

What's the value at the end of Year 3 of the following CF stream if the quoted interest rate is 10%, compounded semiannually?

■ Payments occur annually, but compounding occurs each 6 months.

■ So we can't use normal annuity valuation techniques.

1st Method: Compound Each CF

$FVA_3 = \$100(1.05)^4 + \$100(1.05)^2 + \$100$
$= \$331.80.$

2nd Method: Treat as an Annuity

Could you find FV with a financial calculator?

Yes, by following these steps:

a. Find the EAR for the quoted rate:

$$EAR = \left(1 + \frac{0.10}{2}\right)^2 - 1 = 10.25\%.$$

Or, to find EAR with a calculator:

NOM% = 10.

P/YR = 2.

EFF% = 10.25.

---

b. The cash flow stream is an annual
   annuity. Find k_{Nom} (annual) whose
   EFF% = 10.25%. In calculator,

   EFF% = 10.25
   P/YR = 1
   NOM% = 10.25

c.

INPUTS	3	10.25	0	-100	
	N	I/YR	PV	PMT	FV
OUTPUT					331.80

What's the PV of this stream?

Amortization

Construct an **amortization schedule** for a $1,000, 10% annual rate loan with 3 equal payments.

Step 1: Find the required annual payments.

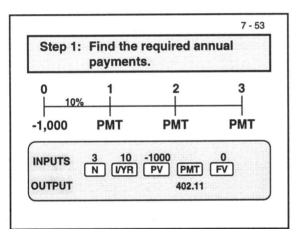

INPUTS	3	10	-1000		0
	N	I/YR	PV	PMT	FV
OUTPUT				402.11	

Step 2: Find the interest paid in Year 1.

$INT_t = Beg\ bal_t\ (i)$
$INT_1 = \$1,000(0.10) = \boxed{\$100.}$

Step 3: Find repayment of principal in Year 1.

$Repmt = PMT - INT$
$= \$402.11 - \$100$
$= \boxed{\$302.11.}$

Step 4: Find ending balance after Year 1.

End bal = Beg bal – Repmt
= $1,000 – $302.11 = $697.89.

Repeat steps 2-4 for Years 2 and 3 to complete the amortization table.

YR	BEG BAL	PMT	INT	PRIN PMT	END BAL
1	$1,000	$402	$100	$302	$698
2	698	402	70	332	366
3	366	402	37	366	0
TOT		1,206.34	206.34	1,000	

Interest declines. Tax implications.

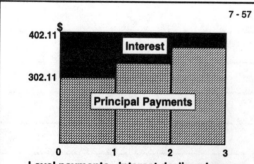

Level payments. Interest declines because outstanding balance declines. Lender earns 10% on loan outstanding, which is falling.

---

7 - 58

■ Amortization tables are widely used--
for home mortgages, auto loans,
business loans, retirement plans, etc.
They are very important!

■ Financial calculators (and
spreadsheets) are great for setting up
amortization tables.

EXAM-TYPE PROBLEMS

7-1. Which of the following statements is most correct?

    a. The first payment under a 3-year, annual payment, amortized loan for $1,000 will include a *smaller* percentage (or fraction) of the payment as interest if the interest rate is 5 percent than if it is 10 percent.

    b. If you are lending money, then, based on effective interest rates, you should prefer to lend at a 10 percent nominal, or quoted, rate but with semiannual payments, rather than at a 10.1 percent nominal rate with annual payments. However, as a borrower you should prefer the annual payment loan.

    c. The value of a perpetuity (say for $100 per year) will approach infinity as the interest rate used to evaluate the perpetuity approaches zero.

    d. Statements a, b, and c are true.

    e. Only statements b and c are true.

7-2. You want to buy a new BMW sports car on your 27th birthday. You have priced these cars and found that they currently sell for $25,000. You believe that the price will increase by 10 percent per year until you are ready to buy one. You can presently invest to earn 14 percent. If you just turned 20 years old, how much must you invest at the end of each of the next 7 years to be able to purchase the BMW in 7 years? ($4,540.15)

7-3. On January 1, 2002, a graduate student developed a 5-year financial plan that would provide enough money at the end of her graduate work (January 1, 2007) to open a business of her own. Her plan was to deposit $8,000 per year for 5 years, starting immediately, into an account paying 10 percent compounded annually. Her activities proceeded according to plan except that at the end of her third year (1/1/05) she withdrew $5,000 to take a Caribbean cruise, at the end of the fourth year (1/1/06) she withdrew $5,000 to buy a used Prelude, and at the end of the fifth year (1/1/07) she had to withdraw $5,000 for her dissertation to be typed. Her account, at the end of the fifth year, was less than the amount she had originally planned on by how much? ($16,550)

7-4. You have just taken out a 30-year, $120,000 mortgage on your new home. This mortgage is to be repaid in 360 equal end-of-month installments. If each of the monthly installments is $1,500, what is the effective annual interest rate on this mortgage? (15.87%)

7-5. Assume that your father is now 50 years old, that he plans to retire in 10 years, and that he expects to live for 25 years after he retires, that is, until he is 85. He wants a fixed retirement income that has the same purchasing power at the time he retires as $40,000 has today. (He realizes that the real value of his retirement income will decline year by year after he retires.) His retirement income will begin the day he retires, 10 years from today, and he will then get 24 additional annual payments. Inflation is expected to be 5 percent per year from today forward; he currently has $100,000 saved up; and he expects to earn a return on his savings of 8 percent per year, annual compounding. To the nearest dollar, how much must he save during each of the next 10 years (with deposits being made at the end of each year) to meet his retirement goal? ($36,950)

7-6. An investment pays you 10 percent interest, compounded quarterly.

a. What is the periodic rate of interest? (2.5%)

b. What is the nominal rate of interest? (10%)

c. What is the effective annual rate of interest? (10.38%)

8-23 Robert Black and Carol Alvarez are vice-presidents of Western Money Management and codirectors of the company's pension fund management division. A major new client, the California League of Cities, has requested that Western present an investment seminar to the mayors of the represented cities, and Black and Alvarez, who will make the actual presentation, have asked you to help them by answering the following questions.

a. What are the key features of a bond?

b. What are call provisions and sinking fund provisions? Do these provisions make bonds more or less risky?

c. How is the value of any asset whose value is based on expected future cash flows determined?

d. How is the value of a bond determined? What is the value of a 10-year, $1,000 par value bond with a 10 percent annual coupon if its required rate of return is 10 percent?

e. (1) What would be the value of the bond described in part d if, just after it had been issued, the expected inflation rate rose by 3 percentage points, causing investors to require a 13 percent return? Would we now have a discount or a premium bond? (If you do not have a financial calculator, $PVIF_{13\%,10} = 0.2946$; $PVIFA_{13\%,10} = 5.4262$.)

   (2) What would happen to the bonds' value if inflation fell, and k_d declined to 7 percent? Would we now have a premium or a discount bond?

   (3) What would happen to the value of the 10-year bond over time if the required rate of return remained at 13 percent, or if it remained at 7 percent? (Hint: With a financial calculator, enter PMT, I, FV, and N, and then change (override) N to see what happens to the PV as the bond approaches maturity.)

f. (1) What is the yield to maturity on a 10-year, 9 percent, annual coupon, $1,000 par value bond that sells for $887.00? That sells for $1,134.20? What does the fact that a bond sells at a discount or at a premium tell you about the relationship between k_d and the bond's coupon rate?

(2) What are the total return, the current yield, and the capital gains yield for the discount bond? (Assume the bond is held to maturity and the company does not default on the bond.)

g. What is *interest rate (or price) risk*? Which bond has more interest rate risk, an annual payment 1-year bond or a 10-year bond? Why?

h. What is *reinvestment rate risk*? Which has more reinvestment rate risk, a 1-year bond or a 10-year bond?

i. How does the equation for valuing a bond change if semiannual payments are made? Find the value of a 10-year, semiannual payment, 10 percent coupon bond if nominal k_d = 13%. (Hint: $PVIF_{6.5\%,20}$ = 0.2838 and $PVIFA_{6.5\%,20}$ = 11.0185.)

j. Suppose you could buy, for $1,000, either a 10 percent, 10-year, annual payment bond or a 10 percent, 10-year, semiannual payment bond. They are equally risky. Which would you prefer? If $1,000 is the proper price for the semiannual bond, what is the equilibrium price for the annual payment bond?

k. Suppose a 10-year, 10 percent, semiannual coupon bond with a par value of $1,000 is currently selling for $1,135.90, producing a nominal yield to maturity of 8 percent. However, the bond can be called after 4 years for a price of $1,050.

(1) What is the bond's *nominal yield to call (YTC)*?

(2) If you bought this bond, do you think you would be more likely to earn the YTM or the YTC? Why?

l. Does the yield to maturity represent the promised or expected return on the bond?

m. These bonds were rated AA- by S&P. Would you consider these bonds investment grade or junk bonds?

n. What factors determine a company's bond rating?

o. If this firm were to default on the bonds, would the company be immediately liquidated? Would the bondholders be assured of receiving all of their promised payments?

CHAPTER 8
Bonds and Their Valuation

- Key features of bonds
- Bond valuation
- Measuring yield
- Assessing risk

Key Features of a Bond

1. **Par value:** Face amount; paid at maturity. Assume $1,000.

2. **Coupon interest rate:** Stated interest rate. Multiply by par to get $ of interest. Generally fixed.

3. **Maturity:** Years until bond must be repaid. Declines.

4. **Issue date:** Date when bond was issued.

How does adding a "call provision" affect a bond?

- ■ Issuer can refund if rates decline. That helps the issuer but hurts the investor.
- ■ Therefore, borrowers are willing to pay more, and lenders require more, on callable bonds.
- ■ Most bonds have a deferred call and a declining call premium.

What is a sinking fund?

- ■ Provision to pay off a loan over its life rather than all at maturity.
- ■ Similar to amortization on a term loan.
- ■ Reduces risk to investor, shortens average maturity.
- ■ But not good for investors if rates decline after issuance.

Sinking funds are generally handled in 2 ways

1. Call x% at par per year for sinking fund purposes.
2. Buy bonds on open market.

Company would call if k_d is below the coupon rate and bond sells at a premium. Use open market purchase if k_d is above coupon rate and bond sells at a discount.

Financial Asset Values

$$PV = \frac{CF_1}{(1+k)^1} + \frac{CF_2}{(1+k)^2} + \dots + \frac{CF_n}{(1+k)^n}.$$

■ The discount rate (k_I) is the opportunity cost of capital, i.e., the rate that could be earned on alternative investments of equal risk.

$$k_I = k^* + IP + LP + MRP + DRP.$$

What's the value of a 10-year, 10% coupon bond if k_d = 10%?

$$V_B = \frac{\$100}{(1+k_d)^1} + \dots + \frac{\$100}{(1+k_d)^{10}} + \frac{\$1,000}{(1+k_d)^{10}}$$

$$= \$90.91 + \dots + \$38.55 + \$385.54$$
$$= \$1,000.$$

The bond consists of a 10-year, 10% annuity of $100/year plus a $1,000 lump sum at t = 10:

PV annuity	=	$ 614.46
PV maturity value	=	385.54
PV bond	=	$1,000.00

INPUTS	10	10		100	1000
	N	I/YR	PV	PMT	FV
OUTPUT			-1,000		

What would happen if expected inflation rose by 3%, causing k = 13%?

INPUTS	10	13		100	1000
	N	I/YR	PV	PMT	FV
OUTPUT			-837.21		

When k_d rises, <u>above</u> the coupon rate, the bond's value falls <u>below</u> par, so it sells at a <u>discount</u>.

What would happen if inflation fell, and k_d declined to 7%?

INPUTS	10	7		100	1000
	N	I/YR	PV	PMT	FV
OUTPUT			-1,210.71		

Price rises above par, and bond sells at a premium, if coupon > k_d.

The bond was issued 20 years ago and now has 10 years to maturity. What would happen to its value over time if the required rate of return remained at 10%, or at 13%, or at 7%?

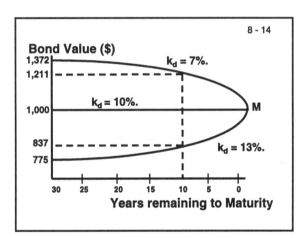

- At maturity, the value of any bond must equal its par value.
- The value of a premium bond would decrease to $1,000.
- The value of a discount bond would increase to $1,000.
- A par bond stays at $1,000 if k_d remains constant.

What is the "yield to maturity"?

- YTM is the rate of return earned on a bond held to maturity. Also called the "promised yield."

What's the YTM on a 10-year, 9% annual coupon, $1,000 par value bond that sells for $887?

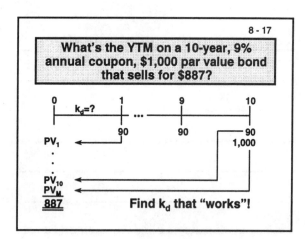

Find k_d that "works"!

Find k_d

$$V_B = \frac{INT}{(1+k_d)^1} + \cdots + \frac{INT}{(1+k_d)^N} + \frac{M}{(1+k_d)^N}$$

$$887 = \frac{90}{(1+k_d)^1} + \cdots + \frac{90}{(1+k_d)^{10}} + \frac{1,000}{(1+k_d)^{10}}$$

INPUTS	10		-887	90	1000
	[N]	[I/YR]	[PV]	[PMT]	[FV]
OUTPUT		10.91			

- If coupon rate < k_d, discount.
- If coupon rate = k_d, par bond.
- If coupon rate > k_d, premium.
- If k_d rises, price falls.
- Price = par at maturity.

Find YTM if price were $1,134.20.

INPUTS	10		-1134.2	90	1000
	N	I/YR	PV	PMT	FV
OUTPUT		7.08			

Sells at a premium. Because
coupon = 9% > k_d = 7.08%,
bond's value > par.

Definitions

Current yield = $\dfrac{\text{Annual coupon pmt}}{\text{Current price}}$.

Capital gains yield = $\boxed{\dfrac{\text{Change in price}}{\text{Beginning price}}}$.

$\substack{\text{Exp total} \\ \text{return}}$ = YTM = $\boxed{\substack{\text{Exp} \\ \text{Curr yld}}}$ + $\substack{\text{Exp cap} \\ \text{gains yld}}$.

Find current yield and capital gains yield for a 9%, 10-year bond when the bond sells for $887 and YTM = 10.91%.

Current yield $= \dfrac{\$90}{\$887}$

$= 0.1015 = 10.15\%.$

YTM = Current yield + Capital gains yield.

Cap gains yield = YTM − Current yield
   = 10.91% − 10.15%
   = 0.76%.

Could also find value in Years 1 and 2, get difference, and divide by value in Year 1. Same answer.

What's interest rate (or price) risk? Does a 1-year or 10-year 10% bond have more risk?

Interest rate risk: Rising k_d causes bond's price to fall.

k_d	1-year	Change	10-year	Change
5%	$1,048		$1,386	
		+4.8%		+38.6%
10%	1,000		1,000	
		−4.4%		−25.1%
15%	956		749	

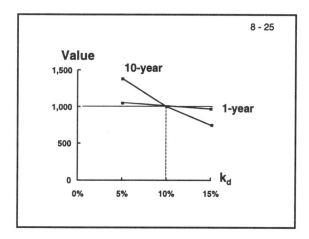

Value

1,500 — 10-year

1,000 — 1-year

500

0 — k_d

0% 5% 10% 15%

What is reinvestment rate risk?

The risk that CFs will have to be reinvested in the future at lower rates, reducing income.

Illustration: Suppose you just won $500,000 playing the lottery. You'll invest the money and live off the interest. You buy a 1-year bond with a YTM of 10%.

Year 1 income = $50,000. At year-end get back $500,000 to reinvest.

If rates fall to 3%, income will drop from $50,000 to $15,000. Had you bought 30-year bonds, income would have remained constant.

■ **Long-term bonds:** High interest rate risk, low reinvestment rate risk.

■ **Short-term bonds:** Low interest rate risk, high reinvestment rate risk.

■ **Nothing is riskless!**

Do all bonds of the same maturity have the same price and reinvestment rate risk?

No, low coupon bonds have less reinvestment rate risk but more price risk than high coupon bonds.

Semiannual Bonds

1. Multiply years by 2 to get periods = 2n.
2. Divide nominal rate by 2 to get periodic rate = $k_d/2$.
3. Divide annual INT by 2 to get PMT = INT/2.

INPUTS	2n	$k_d/2$	OK	INT/2	OK
	N	I/YR	PV	PMT	FV
OUTPUT					

Find the value of 10-year, 10% coupon, semiannual bond if k_d = 13%.

```
                2(10)   13/2        100/2
INPUTS           20      6.5          50      1000
                [N]    [I/YR]  [PV]  [PMT]   [FV]
OUTPUT                        -834.72
```

You could buy, for $1,000, either a 10%, 10-year, annual payment bond or an equally risky 10%, 10-year semiannual bond. Which would you prefer?

The semiannual bond's EFF% is:

$$EFF\% = \left(1+\frac{i_{Nom}}{m}\right)^m - 1 = \left(1+\frac{0.10}{2}\right)^2 - 1 = 10.25\%.$$

10.25% > 10% EFF% on annual bond, so buy semiannual bond.

If $1,000 is the proper price for the semiannual bond, what is the proper price for the annual payment bond?

■ Semiannual bond has k_{Nom} = 10%, with EFF% = 10.25%. Should earn same EFF% on annual payment bond, so:

```
INPUTS    10    10.25        100    1000
          [N]  [I/YR]  [PV]  [PMT]  [FV]
OUTPUT                -984.80
```

■ At a price of $984.80, the annual and semiannual bonds would be in equilibrium, because investors would earn EFF% = 10.25% on either bond.

A 10-year, 10% semiannual coupon, $1,000 par value bond is selling for $1,135.90 with an 8% yield to maturity. It can be called after 4 years at $1,050.

What's the bond's nominal yield to call (YTC)?

INPUTS	8		-1135.9	50	1050
	N	I/YR	PV	PMT	FV
OUTPUT	3.568 x 2 = 7.137%				

---

k_{Nom} = 7.137% is the rate brokers would quote. Could also calculate EFF% to call:

EFF% = $(1.03568)^2 - 1$ = 7.26%.

This rate could be compared to monthly mortgages, etc.

If you bought bonds, would you be more likely to earn YTM or YTC?

- Coupon rate = 10% vs. YTC = k_d = 7.137%. Could raise money by selling new bonds which pay 7.137%.
- Could thus replace bonds that pay $100/year with bonds that pay only $71.37/year.
- Investors should expect a call, hence YTC = 7.1%, not YTM = 8%.

- In general, if a bond sells at a premium, then (1) coupon > k_d, so (2) a call is likely.
- So, expect to earn:
  - YTC on premium bonds.
  - YTM on par & discount bonds.

- Disney recently issued 100-year bonds with a YTM of 7.5%--this represents the promised return. The expected return was less than 7.5% when the bonds were issued.
- If issuer defaults, investors receive less than the promised return. Therefore, the expected return on corporate and municipal bonds is less than the promised return.

Bond Ratings Provide One Measure of Default Risk

	Investment Grade				Junk Bonds			
Moody's	Aaa	Aa	A	Baa	Ba	B	Caa	C
S&P	AAA	AA	A	BBB	BB	B	CCC	D

What factors affect default risk and bond ratings?

- Financial performance
  - Debt ratio
  - TIE ratio
  - Current ratio

- Provisions in the bond contract
  - Secured vs. unsecured debt
  - Senior vs. subordinated debt
  - Guarantee provisions
  - Sinking fund provisions
  - Debt maturity

■ Other factors
- ● Earnings stability
- ● Regulatory environment
- ● Potential product liability
- ● Accounting policies

Top Ten Largest U.S. Corporate Bond Financings, as of July 1999

Issuer	Date	Amount
Ford Motor Co.	July 1999	$8.6 billion
AT&T	Mar 1999	$8.0 billion
RJR Holdings	May 1989	$6.1 billion
WorldCom	Aug 1998	$6.1 billion
Sprint	Nov 1998	$5.0 billion

Bankruptcy

■ Two main chapters of Federal Bankruptcy Act:
- ● Chapter 11, Reorganization
- ● Chapter 7, Liquidation

■ Typically, company wants Chapter 11, creditors may prefer Chapter 7.

8 - 46

■ If company can't meet its obligations, it files under Chapter 11. That stops creditors from foreclosing, taking assets, and shutting down the business.

■ Company has 120 days to file a reorganization plan.
- Court appoints a "trustee" to supervise reorganization.
- Management usually stays in control.

_____

_____

_____

_____

_____

_____

_____

8 - 47

■ Company must demonstrate in its reorganization plan that it is "worth more alive than dead."

Otherwise, judge will order liquidation under Chapter 7.

_____

_____

_____

_____

_____

_____

_____

8 - 48

■ If the company is liquidated, here's the payment priority:
1. Secured creditors from sales of secured assets.
2. Trustee's costs
3. Wages, subject to limits
4. Taxes
5. Unfunded pension liabilities
6. Unsecured creditors
7. Preferred stock
8. Common stock

_____

_____

_____

_____

_____

_____

_____

■ In a liquidation, unsecured creditors generally get zero. This makes them more willing to participate in reorganization even though their claims are greatly scaled back.

■ Various groups of creditors vote on the reorganization plan. If both the majority of the creditors and the judge approve, company "emerges" from bankruptcy with lower debts, reduced interest charges, and a chance for success.

_____

_____

_____

_____

_____

_____

_____

EXAM-TYPE PROBLEMS

8-1. Gator Services Unlimited (GSU) needs to raise $25 million in new debt capital. GSU's currently outstanding bonds have a $1,000 par value, an 8 percent coupon rate, pay interest semiannually, and have 30 years remaining to maturity. The bonds are callable after 5 years at a price of $1,080, and currently sell at a price of $676.77. Right now, the yield curve is flat and is expected to remain flat for a while. The risk on GSU's new bonds is the same as for its old bonds. On the basis of these data, what is the best estimate of GSU's nominal interest rate on new bonds? (12%)

8-2. Florida Financial Corporation (FFC) purchases packages of guaranteed student loans from banks for its portfolio. FFC is considering a package with the following characteristics. The securities, which are similar to bonds, have a $1,000 par value, pay 8 percent interest semiannually for 5 years, and then pay a stepped-up interest rate of 10 percent semiannually for the next 7 years. The maturity value is $1,000, paid at the end of 12 years. FFC's alternatives to this investment are 9 percent coupon bonds, selling at par of $1,000, which pay interest quarterly. Assuming that the investments are of similar risk, how much should FFC be willing to pay for the student loan package? ($985.97)

8-3. Trickle Corporation's 12 percent coupon rate, semiannual payment, $1,000 par value bonds that mature in 25 years, are callable at a price of $1,080 five years from now. The bonds currently sell for $1,230.51 in the market, and the yield curve is flat. Assuming that the yield curve is expected to remain flat, what is Trickle's most likely *before-tax cost* of debt if it issues new bonds today? (7.70%)

8-4. Recycler Battery Corporation (RBC) issued zero coupon bonds 5 years ago at a price of $214.50 per bond. RBC's zeros had a 20-year original maturity, and a $1,000 par value. The bonds were callable 10 years after the issue date at a price 7 percent over their accrued value on the call date. If the bonds sell for $239.39 in the market today, what annual rate of return should an investor who buys the bonds today expect to earn on them? (Hint: Material covered in Appendix 8A.) (10%)

8-5. Suppose a new company decides to raise its initial $200 million of capital as $100 million of common equity and $100 million of long-term debt. By an iron-clad provision in its charter, the company can never borrow any more money. Which of the following statements is most correct?

a. If the debt were raised by issuing $50 million of debentures and $50 million of first mortgage bonds, we could be absolutely certain that the firm's total interest expense would be lower than if the debt were raised by issuing $100 million of debentures.

---

b. If the debt were raised by issuing $50 million of debentures and $50 million of first mortgage bonds, we could be absolutely certain that the firm's total interest expense would be lower than if the debt were raised by issuing $100 million of first mortgage bonds.

c. The higher the percentage of total debt represented by debentures, the greater the risk of, and hence the interest rate on, the debentures.

d. The higher the percentage of total debt represented by mortgage bonds, the riskier both types of bonds will be, and, consequently, the higher the firms' total dollar interest charges will be.

e. In this situation, we cannot tell for sure how, or whether, the firm's total interest expense on the $100 million of debt would be affected by the mix of debentures versus first mortgage bonds. Interest rates on the two types of bonds would vary as their percentages were changed, but the result might well be such that the firm's total interest charges would not be affected materially by the mix between the two.

8-6. Which of the following statements is most correct?

a. Because bonds can generally be called only at a premium, meaning that the bondholder will enjoy a capital gain, including a call provision (other than a sinking fund call) in the indenture increases the value of the bond and lowers the bond's required rate of return.

b. You are considering two bonds. Both are rated AA, both mature in 20 years, both have a 10 percent coupon, and both are offered to you at their $1,000 par value. However, Bond X has a sinking fund while Bond Y does not. This is probably not an equilibrium situation, as Bond X, which has the sinking fund, would generally be expected to have a higher yield than Bond Y.

c. A sinking fund provides for the orderly retirement of a debt (or preferred stock) issue. Sinking funds generally force the firm to call a percentage of the issue each year. However, the call price for sinking fund purposes is generally higher than the call price for refunding purposes.

d. Zero coupon bonds are bought primarily by pension funds and other tax-exempt investors because they avoid the tax that non-tax exempt investors must pay on the accrued value each year.

e. All of the above statements are false.

8-7. Research Technologies' noncallable bonds have 10 years remaining to maturity. The bonds have a face value of $1,000, a yield to maturity of 12 percent, pay interest semiannually, and have a 10 percent coupon rate. What is their current yield? (11.30%)

9-28   Robert Balik and Carol Kiefer are senior vice-presidents of the Mutual of Chicago Insurance Company.   They are co-directors of the company's pension fund management division, with Balik having responsibility for fixed income securities (primarily bonds) and Kiefer being responsible for equity investments. A major new client, the California League of Cities, has requested that Mutual of Chicago present an investment seminar to the mayors of the represented cities, and Balik and Kiefer, who will make the actual presentation, have asked you to help them.

To illustrate the common stock valuation process, Balik and Kiefer have asked you to analyze the Bon Temps Company, an employment agency that supplies word processor operators and computer programmers to businesses with temporarily heavy workloads. You are to answer the following questions.

a.   Describe briefly the legal rights and privileges of common stockholders.

b.   (1) Write out a formula that can be used to value any stock, regardless of its dividend pattern.

   (2) What is a constant growth stock? How are constant growth stocks valued?

   (3) What happens if a company has a constant g that exceeds its k_s? Will many stocks have expected $g > k_s$ in the short run (that is, for the next few years)? In the long run (that is, forever)?

c.   Assume that Bon Temps has a beta coefficient of 1.2, that the risk-free rate (the yield on T-bonds) is 7 percent, and that the required rate of return on the market is 12 percent. What is the required rate of return on the firm's stock?

d.   Assume that Bon Temps is a constant growth company whose last dividend (D_0, which was paid yesterday) was $2.00 and whose dividend is expected to grow indefinitely at a 6 percent rate.

   (1) What is the firm's expected dividend stream over the next 3 years?

   (2) What is the firm's current stock price?

   (3) What is the stock's expected value 1 year from now?

   (4) What are the expected dividend yield, the capital gains yield, and the total return during the first year?

e.   Now assume that the stock is currently selling at $30.29. What is the expected rate of return on the stock?

f.   What would the stock price be if its dividends were expected to have zero growth?

g.   Now assume that Bon Temps is expected to experience supernormal growth of 30 percent for the next 3 years, then to return to its long-run constant growth rate of 6 percent. What is the stock's value under these conditions? What is its expected dividend yield and capital gains yield in Year 1? Year 4?

h.   Suppose Bon Temps is expected to experience zero growth during the first 3 years and then to resume its steady-state growth of 6 percent in the fourth year. What is the stock's value now? What is its expected dividend yield and its capital gains yield in Year 1? Year 4?

i.   Finally, assume that Bon Temps' earnings and dividends are expected to decline by a constant 6 percent per year, that is, $g = -6\%$. Why would anyone be willing to buy such a stock, and at what price should it sell? What would be the dividend yield and capital gains yield in each year?

j.   Bon Temps embarks on an aggressive expansion that requires additional capital. Management decides to finance the expansion by borrowing $40 million and by halting dividend payments to increase retained earnings. The projected free cash flows for the next three years are -$5 million, $10 million, and $20 million. After the third year, free cash flow is projected to grow at a constant 6 percent. The overall cost of capital is 10 percent. What is Bon Temps' total value? If it has 10 million shares of stock and $40 million total debt, what is the price per share?

k.   What does market equilibrium mean?

l.   If equilibrium does not exist, how will it be established?

m.   What is the Efficient Markets Hypothesis, what are its three forms, and what are its implications?

n.   Phyfe Company recently issued preferred stock. It pays an annual dividend of $5, and the issue price was $50 per share. What is the expected return to an investor on this preferred stock?

CHAPTER 9
Stocks and Their Valuation

- Features of common stock
- Determining common stock values
- Efficient markets
- Preferred stock

Facts about Common Stock

- Represents ownership.
- Ownership implies control.
- Stockholders elect directors.
- Directors elect management.
- Management's goal: Maximize the stock price.

Social/Ethical Question

Should management be equally concerned about employees, customers, suppliers, and "the public," or just the stockholders?

In an enterprise economy, management should work for stockholders subject to constraints (environmental, fair hiring, etc.) and competition.

When is a stock sale an initial public offering (IPO)?

A firm "goes public" through an IPO when the stock is first offered to the public.

Biggest IPOs of 2000

Issuer	Proceeds from sale
AT&T Wireless	$9.03 billion
Infineon Technologies	$2.72 billion
Metropolitan Life Ins. Co.	$2.50 billion
TyCom	$2.88 billion
Genuity	$1.91 billion

Average Initial Returns on IPOs in Various Countries

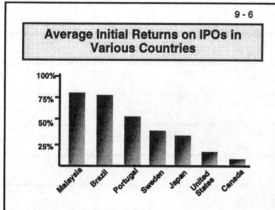

Different Approaches for Valuing Common Stock

- Dividend growth model
- Free cash flow method
- Using the multiples of comparable firms

Stock Value = PV of Dividends

$$\hat{P}_0 = \frac{D_1}{(1+k_s)^1} + \frac{D_2}{(1+k_s)^2} + \frac{D_3}{(1+k_s)^3} + \ldots + \frac{D_\infty}{(1+k_s)^\infty}.$$

What is a constant growth stock?

One whose dividends are expected to grow forever at a constant rate, g.

For a Constant Growth Stock

$$D_1 = D_0(1 + g)^1$$
$$D_2 = D_0(1 + g)^2$$
$$D_t = D_t(1 + g)^t$$

If g is constant, then:

$$\hat{P}_0 = \frac{D_0(1 + g)}{k_s - g} = \frac{D_1}{k_s - g}.$$

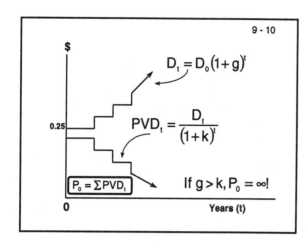

$$D_t = D_0(1+g)^t$$

$$PVD_t = \frac{D_t}{(1+k)^t}$$

$$P_0 = \Sigma PVD_t$$

If $g > k, P_0 = \infty!$

What happens if $g > k_s$?

$$\hat{P}_0 = \frac{D_1}{k_s - g} \text{ requires } k_s > g.$$

- If $k_s < g$, get negative stock price, which is nonsense.

- We can't use model unless (1) $k_s > g$ and (2) g is expected to be constant forever.

Assume beta = 1.2, k_{RF} = 7%, and k_M = 12%. What is the required rate of return on the firm's stock?

Use the SML to calculate k_s:

$$k_s = k_{RF} + (k_M - k_{RF})b_{Firm}$$
$$= 7\% + (12\% - 7\%)(1.2)$$
$$= 13\%.$$

D_0 was $2.00 and g is a constant 6%. Find the expected dividends for the next 3 years, and their PVs. k_s = 13%.

D_0 = 2.00 2.12   2.247   2.382
13%
1.8761
1.7599
1.6509

What's the stock's market value? D_0 = 2.00, k_s = 13%, g = 6%.

Constant growth model:

$$P_0 = \frac{D_1}{k_s - g} = \frac{\$2.12}{0.13 - 0.06}$$

$$= \frac{\$2.12}{0.07} = \$30.29.$$

What is the stock's market value one year from now, $\hat{P}_1$?

■ D_1 will have been paid, so expected dividends are D_2, D_3, D_4 and so on. Thus,

$$\hat{P}_1 = \frac{D_2}{k_s - g} = \frac{\$2.247}{0.13 - 0.06}$$

$$= \$32.10.$$

Could also find $\hat{P}_1$ as follows:

$$\hat{P}_1 = P_0(1.06) = \$32.10.$$

Find the expected dividend yield, capital gains yield, and total return during the first year.

Dividend yld $= \dfrac{D_1}{P_0} = \dfrac{\$2.12}{\$30.29} = 7.0\%$.

Cap gains yld $= \dfrac{\hat{P}_1 - P_0}{P_0} = \dfrac{\$32.10 - \$30.29}{\$30.29}$
$= 6.0\%$.

Total return $= 7.0\% + 6.0\% = 13.0\%$.

Rearrange model to rate of return form:

$$\hat{P}_0 = \dfrac{D_1}{k_s - g} \text{ to } \hat{k}_s = \dfrac{D_1}{P_0} + g.$$

Then, $\hat{k}_s = \$2.12/\$30.29 + 0.06$
$= 0.07 + 0.06 = 13\%$.

What would $\hat{P}_0$ be if g = 0?

The dividend stream would be a perpetuity.

```
0    13%    1        2        3
|-----------|--------|--------|----->  ...
          2.00     2.00     2.00
```

$\hat{P}_0 = \dfrac{PMT}{k} = \dfrac{\$2.00}{0.13} = \$15.38$.

If we have supernormal growth of 30% for 3 years, then a long-run constant $g = 6\%$, what is $\hat{P}_0$? k is still 13%.

- Can no longer use constant growth model.
- However, growth becomes constant after 3 years.

Nonconstant growth followed by constant growth:

$$\hat{P}_3 = \frac{4.658}{0.13 - 0.06} = \$66.54$$

What is the expected dividend yield and capital gains yield at t = 0? At t = 4?

$$\text{Div. yield}_0 = \frac{\$2.60}{\$54.11} = 4.81\%.$$

$$\text{Cap. gain}_0 = 13.00\% - 4.81\% = 8.19\%.$$

- During nonconstant growth, D/P and capital gains yield are not constant, and capital gains yield is not equal to g.

- After t = 3, g = constant = 6% = capital gains yield; k = 13%; so D/P = 13% − 6% = 7%.

Suppose g = 0 for t = 1 to 3, and then g is a constant 6%. What is $\hat{P}_0$?

$$\hat{P}_3 = \frac{2.12}{0.07} = 30.29.$$

What is D/P and capital gains yield at t = 0 and at t = 3?

t = 0: $\dfrac{D_1}{P_0} = \dfrac{\$2.00}{\$25.72} = 7.78\%.$

CGY = 13% − 7.78% = 5.22%.

t = 3: Now have constant growth with g = capital gains yield = 6% and D/P = 7%.

If g = -6%, would anyone buy the stock? If so, at what price?

Firm still has earnings and still pays dividends, so $P_0 > 0$:

$$\hat{P}_0 = \frac{D_1}{k_s - g} = \frac{D_0(1 + g)}{k_s - g}$$

$$= \frac{\$2.00(0.94)}{0.13 - (-0.06)} = \frac{\$1.88}{0.19} = \$9.89.$$

What is the annual D/P and capital gains yield?

Capital gains yield = g = -6.0%,

Dividend yield= 13.0% − (-6.0%) = 19%.

D/P and cap. gains yield are constant, with high dividend yield (19%) offsetting negative capital gains yield.

Free Cash Flow Method

■ The free cash flow method suggests that the value of the entire firm equals the present value of the firm's free cash flows (calculated on an after-tax basis).

■ Recall that the free cash flow in any given year can be calculated as:

NOPAT − Net capital investment.

Using the Free Cash Flow Method

- Once the value of the firm is estimated, an estimate of the stock price can be found as follows:
  - MV of common stock (market capitalization) = MV of firm − MV of debt and preferred stock.
  - $\hat{P}$ = MV of common stock/# of shares.

Issues Regarding the Free Cash Flow Method

- Free cash flow method is often preferred to the dividend growth model--particularly for the large number of companies that don't pay a dividend, or for whom it is hard to forecast dividends.

(More...)

FCF Method Issues (Continued)

- Similar to the dividend growth model, the free cash flow method generally assumes that at some point in time, the growth rate in free cash flow will become constant.
- Terminal value represents the value of the firm at the point in which growth becomes constant.

FCF estimates for the next 3 years are -\$5, \$10, and \$20 million, after which the FCF is expected to grow at 6%. The overall firm cost of capital is 10%.

$$530 = \frac{\boxed{21.20}}{0.04} = *TV_3$$

*TV_3 represents the terminal value of the firm, at t = 3.

-4.545
8.264
15.026
398.197
416.942

If the firm has \$40 million in debt and has 10 million shares of stock, what is the price per share?

Value of equity = Total value − Value of debt

= \$416.94 − \$40

= \$376.94 million.

Price per share = Value of equity/# of shares

= \$376.94/10

= \$37.69.

Using the Multiples of Comparable Firms to Estimate Stock Price

- Analysts often use the following multiples to value stocks:
  - P/E
  - P/CF
  - P/Sales
  - P/Customer
- Example: Based on comparable firms, estimate the appropriate P/E. Multiply this by expected earnings to back out an estimate of the stock price.

What is market equilibrium?

In equilibrium, stock prices are stable. There is no general tendency for people to buy versus to sell.

In equilibrium, expected returns must equal required returns:

$$\hat{k}_s = D_1/P_0 + g = k_s = k_{RF} + (k_M - k_{RF})b.$$

Expected returns are obtained by estimating dividends and expected capital gains (which can be found using any of the three common stock valuation approaches).

Required returns are obtained from the CAPM.

$$\hat{k}_s = D_1/P_0 + g = k_s = k_{RF} + (k_M - k_{RF})b.$$

How is equilibrium established?

If $\hat{k}_s = \dfrac{D_1}{P_0} + g > k_s$, then

P_0 is "too low" (a bargain).

Buy orders > sell orders;
P_0 bid up; D_1/P_0 falls until
$D_1/P_0 + g = \hat{k}_s = k_s.$

Why do stock prices change?

$$\hat{P}_0 = \frac{D_1}{k_I - g}.$$

1. k_I could change:
   $k_I = k_{RF} + (k_M - k_{RF})b_I.$
   $k_{RF} = k^* + IP.$

2. g could change due to economic or firm situation.

What's the Efficient Market Hypothesis?

EMH: Securities are normally in equilibrium and are "fairly priced." One cannot "beat the market" except through good luck or better information.

1. **Weak-form EMH:**
   Can't profit by looking at past trends. A recent decline is no reason to think stocks will go up (or down) in the future. Evidence supports weak-form EMH, but "technical analysis" is still used.

2. Semistrong-form EMH:

All publicly available information is reflected in stock prices, so doesn't pay to pore over annual reports looking for undervalued stocks. Largely true, but superior analysts can still profit by finding and using new information.

3. Strong-form EMH:

All information, even inside information, is embedded in stock prices. Not true--insiders can gain by trading on the basis of insider information, but that's illegal.

Markets are generally efficient because:

1. 15,000 or so trained analysts; MBAs, CFAs, Technical PhDs.
2. Work for firms like Merrill, Morgan, Prudential, which have a lot of money.
3. Have similar access to data.
4. Thus, news is reflected in P_0 almost instantaneously.

Preferred Stock

- Hybrid security.
- Similar to bonds in that preferred stockholders receive a fixed dividend that must be paid before dividends can be paid on common stock.
- However, unlike interest payments on bonds, companies can omit dividend payments on preferred stock without fear of pushing the firm into bankruptcy.

What's the expected return of preferred stock with V_p = $50 and annual dividend = $5?

$$V_p = \$50 = \frac{\$5}{k_p}.$$

$$\hat{k}_p = \frac{\$5}{\$50} = 0.10 = 10.0\%.$$

EXAM-TYPE PROBLEMS

9-1. Carlson Products, a constant growth company, has a current market (and equilibrium) stock price of $20.00. Carlson's next dividend, D_1, is forecasted to be $2.00, and Carlson is growing at an annual rate of 6 percent. Carlson has a beta coefficient of 1.2, and the required rate of return on the market is 15 percent. As Carlson's financial manager, you have access to insider information concerning a switch in product lines that would not change the growth rate, but would cut Carlson's beta coefficient in half. If you buy the stock at the current market price, what is your expected percentage capital gain? (43%)

9-2. The Hart Mountain Company has recently discovered a new type of kitty litter that is extremely absorbent. It is expected that the firm will experience (beginning now) an unusually high growth rate of 20 percent during the 3-year period it has exclusive rights to the property where the raw material used to make this kitty litter is found. However, beginning with the fourth year the firm's competition will have access to the material, and from that time on, the firm will achieve a normal growth rate of 8 percent annually. During the rapid growth period, the firm's dividend payout ratio will be a relatively low 20 percent to conserve funds for reinvestment. However, the decrease in growth in the fourth year will be accompanied by an increase in the dividend payout to 50 percent. Last year's earnings were $E_0 = \$2.00$ per share, and the firm's required return is 10 percent. What should be the current price of the common stock? ($71.54)

9-3. Which of the following statements is most correct?

a. One of the advantages of common stock financing is that there is no dilution of owner's equity, as there is with debt.

b. If the market price of a stock falls below its book value, the firm can be liquidated, with the book value proceeds then distributed to the shareholders. Thus, a stock's book value per share sets a floor below which the stock's market price is unlikely to fall.

c. The preemptive right gives a firm's preferred stockholders preference to assets over common stockholders in the event the firm is liquidated.

d. All of the above statements are true.

e. All of the above statements are false.

9-4. Bosio Enterprises has preferred stock outstanding that pays a dividend of $8.75 at the end of each year. If the preferred stock's required return is 12.5 percent, for how much does each share of preferred stock sell? ($70)

9-5. Today is December 31, 2001. The following information applies to Harberford Enterprises:

- After-tax, operating income [EBIT$(1 - T)$] for the Year 2002 is expected to be $800 million.
- The company's depreciation expense for the Year 2002 is expected to be $160 million.
- The company's capital expenditures for the Year 2002 are expected to be $320 million.
- No change is expected in the company's net operating working capital.
- The company's free cash flow is expected to grow at a constant rate of 4 percent per year.
- The company's cost of equity is 12 percent.
- The company's WACC is 9 percent.
- The market value of the company's debt is $4.8 billion.
- The company has 320 million shares of stock outstanding.

Using the free cash flow approach, what should the company's stock price be today? ($25)

10-22 Coleman Technologies is considering a major expansion program that has been proposed by the company's information technology group. Before proceeding with the expansion, the company needs to develop an estimate of its cost of capital. Assume that you are an assistant to Jerry Lehman, the financial vice-president. Your first task is to estimate Coleman's cost of capital. Lehman has provided you with the following data, which he believes may be relevant to your task:

1. The firm's tax rate is 40 percent.

2. The current price of Coleman's 12 percent coupon, semiannual payment, noncallable bonds with 15 years remaining to maturity is $1,153.72. Coleman does not use short-term interest-bearing debt on a permanent basis. New bonds would be privately placed with no flotation cost.

3. The current price of the firm's 10 percent, $100 par value, quarterly dividend, perpetual preferred stock is $111.10.

4. Coleman's common stock is currently selling at $50 per share. Its last dividend (D_0) was $4.19, and dividends are expected to grow at a constant rate of 5 percent in the foreseeable future. Coleman's beta is 1.2, the yield on T-bonds is 7 percent, and the market risk premium is estimated to be 6 percent. For the bond-yield-plus-risk-premium approach, the firm uses a 4 percentage point risk premium.

5. Coleman's target capital structure is 30 percent long-term debt, 10 percent preferred stock, and 60 percent common equity.

To structure the task somewhat, Lehman has asked you to answer the following questions.

a. (1) What sources of capital should be included when you estimate Coleman's weighted average cost of capital (WACC)?

   (2) Should the component costs be figured on a before-tax or an after-tax basis?

   (3) Should the costs be historical (embedded) costs or new (marginal) costs?

b. What is the market interest rate on Coleman's debt and its component cost of debt?

c. (1) What is the firm's cost of preferred stock?

(2) Coleman's preferred stock is riskier to investors than its debt, yet the preferred's yield to investors is lower than the yield to maturity on the debt. Does this suggest that you have made a mistake? (Hint: Think about taxes.)

d. (1) Why is there a cost associated with retained earnings?

(2) What is Coleman's estimated cost of common equity using the CAPM approach?

e. What is the estimated cost of common equity using the discounted cash flow (DCF) approach?

f. What is the bond-yield-plus-risk-premium estimate for Coleman's cost of common equity?

g. What is your final estimate for k_s?

h. Explain in words why new common stock has a higher percentage cost than retained earnings.

i. (1) What are two approaches that can be used to account for flotation costs?

(2) Coleman estimates that if it issues new common stock, the flotation cost will be 15 percent. Coleman incorporates the flotation costs into the DCF approach. What is the estimated cost of newly issued common stock, taking into account the flotation cost?

j. What is Coleman's overall, or weighted average, cost of capital (WACC)? Ignore flotation costs.

k. What factors influence Coleman's composite WACC?

l. Should the company use the composite WACC as the hurdle rate for each of its projects?

m. What are three types of project risk? How is each type of risk used?

n. What procedures are used to determine the risk-adjusted cost of capital for a particular project or division? What approaches are used to measure a project's beta?

o. Coleman is interested in establishing a new division, which will focus primarily on developing new Internet-based projects. In trying to determine the cost of capital for this new division, you discover that stand-alone firms involved in similar projects have on average the following characteristics:

- Their capital structure is 40 percent debt and 60 percent common equity.

- Their cost of debt is typically 12 percent.

- The beta is 1.7.

Given this information, what would your estimate be for the division's cost of capital?

CHAPTER 10
The Cost of Capital

- Sources of capital
- Component costs
- WACC
- Adjusting for flotation costs
- Adjusting for risk

What sources of long-term capital do firms use?

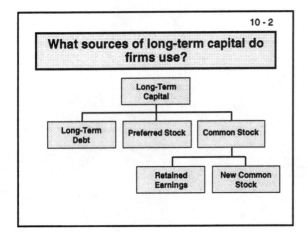

How do you calculate the weighted average cost of capital?

$$WACC = w_d k_d (1 - T) + w_p k_p + w_c k_s.$$

- The w's refer to the capital structure weights.
- The k's refer to the cost of each component.

Should we focus on before-tax or after-tax capital costs?

Stockholders focus on A-T CFs. Therefore, we should focus on A-T capital costs, i.e., use A-T costs in WACC. Only k_d needs adjustment, because interest is deductible.

Should we focus on historical (embedded) costs or new (marginal) costs?

The cost of capital is used primarily to make decisions that involve raising new capital. So, focus on today's marginal costs (for WACC).

How do you determine the weights?

$$WACC = w_d k_d (1 - T) + w_p k_p + w_c k_s.$$

- Use accounting numbers or market value (book vs. market weights)?
- Use actual numbers or target capital structure?

Component Cost of Debt

$$\text{WACC} = w_d k_d (1 - T) + w_p k_p + w_c k_s.$$

- k_d is the marginal cost of debt capital.
- The yield to maturity on outstanding LT debt is often used as a measure of k_d.
- Why tax-adjust, i.e., why $k_d(1 - T)$?

A 15-year, 12% semiannual bond sells for $1,153.72. What is k_d?

INPUTS	30		-1153.72	60	1000
	N	I/YR	PV	PMT	FV
OUTPUT	5.0% x 2 = k_d = 10%				

Component Cost of Debt

- Interest is tax deductible, so

$$k_{d\,AT} = k_{d\,BT}(1 - T)$$
$$= 10\%(1 - 0.40) = 6\%.$$

- Use nominal rate.
- Flotation costs small. Ignore.

Component Cost of Preferred Stock

$$WACC = w_d k_d (1 - T) + w_p k_p + w_c k_s.$$

- k_p is the marginal cost of preferred stock.
- The rate of return investors require on the firm's preferred stock.

What's the cost of preferred stock? $P_p = \$111.10$; 10%Q; Par = $100.

Use this formula:

$$k_p = \frac{D_p}{P_p} = \frac{\$10}{\$111.10} = 0.090 = 9.0\%.$$

Picture of Preferred Stock

```
     0      k_p = ?    1         2        ∞
     |-----------------|---------|---...---|
  -111.1             2.50      2.50      2.50
```

$$\$111.10 = \frac{D_Q}{k_{Per}} = \frac{\$2.50}{k_{Per}}.$$

$$k_{Per} = \frac{\$2.50}{\$111.10} = 2.25\%;$$

$$k_{p(Nom)} = 2.25\%(4) = 9\%.$$

Note:

- Preferred dividends are not tax deductible, so no tax adjustment. Just k_p.
- Nominal k_p is used.
- Our calculation ignores flotation costs.

Is preferred stock more or less risky to investors than debt?

- More risky; company not required to pay preferred dividend.
- However, firms try to pay preferred dividend. Otherwise, (1) cannot pay common dividend, (2) difficult to raise additional funds, (3) preferred stockholders may gain control of firm.

Why is yield on preferred lower than k_d?

- Corporations own most preferred stock, because 70% of preferred dividends are nontaxable to corporations.
- Therefore, preferred often has a lower B-T yield than the B-T yield on debt.
- The A-T yield to an investor, and the A-T cost to the issuer, are higher on preferred than on debt. Consistent with higher risk of preferred.

Example:

$k_p = 9\%$ $k_d = 10\%$ $\boxed{T = 40\%}$

$k_{p,\,AT} = k_p - k_p (1 - 0.7)(T)$
$= 9\% - 9\%(0.3)(0.4) =$ 7.92%.

$\boxed{k_{d,\,AT} = 10\% - 10\%(0.4) = \underline{6.00\%.}}$

A-T Risk Premium on Preferred = $\underline{1.92\%}$.

Component Cost of Equity

$$WACC = w_d k_d (1 - T) + w_p k_p + w_c k_s.$$

- k_s is the marginal cost of common equity using retained earnings.
- The rate of return investors require on the firm's common equity using new equity is k_e.

Why is there a cost for retained earnings?

- Earnings can be reinvested or paid out as dividends.
- Investors could buy other securities, earn a return.
- Thus, there is an opportunity cost if earnings are retained.

■ **Opportunity cost:** The return stockholders could earn on alternative investments of equal risk.

■ **They could buy similar stocks and earn k_s, or company could repurchase its own stock and earn k_s. So, k_s is the cost of retained earnings.**

Three ways to determine cost of common equity, k_s:

1. CAPM: $k_s = k_{RF} + (k_M - k_{RF})b$.

2. DCF: $k_s = D_1/P_0 + g$.

3. Own-Bond-Yield-Plus-Risk Premium: $k_s = k_d + RP$.

What's the cost of common equity based on the CAPM?
k_{RF} = 7%, RP_M = 6%, b = 1.2.

$k_s = k_{RF} + (k_M - k_{RF})b$.

$= 7.0\% + (6.0\%)1.2 = 14.2\%$.

What's the DCF cost of common equity, k_s? Given: $D_0 = \$4.19$; $P_0 = \$50$; $g = 5\%$.

$$k_s = \frac{D_1}{P_0} + g = \frac{D_0(1 + g)}{P_0} + g$$

$$= \frac{\$4.19(1.05)}{\$50} + 0.05$$

$$= 0.088 + 0.05$$

$$= 13.8\%.$$

Suppose the company has been earning 15% on equity (ROE = 15%) and retaining 35% (dividend payout = 65%), and this situation is expected to continue.

What's the expected future g?

Retention growth rate:

$$g = (1 - \text{Payout})(\text{ROE}) = 0.35(15\%)$$
$$= 5.25\%.$$

Here (1 – Payout) = Fraction retained.

Close to g = 5% given earlier. Think of bank account paying 10% with payout = 100%, payout = 0%, and payout = 50%. What's g in each case?

Could DCF methodology be applied if g is not constant?

- YES, nonconstant g stocks are expected to have constant g at some point, generally in 5 to 10 years.
- But calculations get complicated.

Find k_s using the own-bond-yield-plus-risk-premium method. ($k_d = \boxed{10\%},$ RP = 4%.)

$$\boxed{k_s = k_d + RP}$$

$$= \boxed{10.0\%} + 4.0\% = 14.0\%$$

- This RP ≠ CAPM RP.
- Produces ballpark estimate of k_s. Useful check.

What's a reasonable final estimate of k_s?

Method	Estimate
CAPM	14.2%
DCF	13.8%
k_d + RP	14.0%
Average	14.0%

Why is the cost of retained earnings cheaper than the cost of issuing new common stock?

1. When a company issues new common stock they also have to pay flotation costs to the underwriter.
2. Issuing new common stock may send a negative signal to the capital markets, which may depress stock price.

Two approaches that can be used to account for flotation costs:

■ Include the flotation costs as part of the project's up-front cost. This reduces the project's estimated return.

■ Adjust the cost of capital to include flotation costs. This is most commonly done by incorporating flotation costs in the DCF model.

Suppose new common stock had a flotation cost of 15%. What is k_e?

$$k_e = \frac{D_0(1 + g)}{P_0(1 - F)} + g$$

$$= \frac{\$4.19(1.05)}{\$50(1 - 0.15)} + 5.0\%$$

$$= \frac{\$4.40}{\$42.50} + 5.0\% = 15.4\%.$$

Comments about Flotation Costs

- Flotation costs depend on the risk of the firm and the type of capital being raised.
- The flotation costs are highest for common equity. However, since most firms issue equity infrequently, the per-project cost is fairly small.
- We will frequently ignore flotation costs when calculating the WACC.

What's the firm's WACC (ignoring flotation costs)?

$$WACC = w_d k_d(1 - T) + w_p k_p + w_c k_s$$
$$= 0.3(10\%)(0.6) + 0.1(9\%) + 0.6(14\%)$$
$$= 1.8\% + 0.9\% + 8.4\% = 11.1\%.$$

What factors influence a company's composite WACC?

- Market conditions.
- The firm's capital structure and dividend policy.
- The firm's investment policy. Firms with riskier projects generally have a higher WACC.

WACC Estimates for Some Large U.S. Corporations, 1999

Company	WACC
Intel	12.19%
General Electric	12.47
Motorola	11.65
Coca-Cola	12.31
Walt Disney	9.28
AT&T	9.22
Wal-Mart	10.99
Exxon Mobil	8.16
H. J. Heinz	7.78
BellSouth	7.41

Should the company use the composite WACC as the hurdle rate for each of its projects?

- NO! The composite WACC reflects the risk of an average project undertaken by the firm. Therefore, the WACC only represents the "hurdle rate" for a typical project with average risk.
- Different projects have different risks. The project's WACC should be adjusted to reflect the project's risk.

Risk and the Cost of Capital

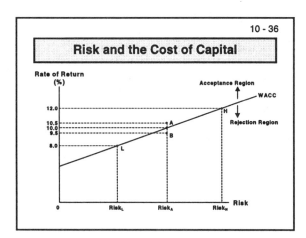

Divisional Cost of Capital

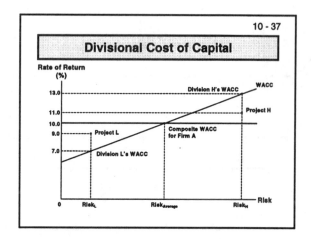

What are the three types of project risk?

- Stand-alone risk
- Corporate risk
- Market risk

How is each type of risk used?

- Market risk is theoretically best in most situations.
- However, creditors, customers, suppliers, and employees are more affected by corporate risk.
- Therefore, corporate risk is also relevant.

What procedures are used to determine the risk-adjusted cost of capital for a particular project or division?

- Subjective adjustments to the firm's composite WACC.
- Attempt to estimate what the cost of capital would be if the project/division were a stand-alone firm. This requires estimating the project's beta.

Methods for Estimating a Project's Beta

1. Pure play. Find several publicly traded companies exclusively in project's business.

   Use average of their betas as proxy for project's beta.

   Hard to find such companies.

2. Accounting beta. Run regression between project's ROA and S&P index ROA.

   Accounting betas are correlated (0.5 – 0.6) with market betas.

   But normally can't get data on new projects' ROAs before the capital budgeting decision has been made.

Find the division's market risk and cost of capital based on the CAPM, given these inputs:

- Target debt ratio = 40%.
- k_d = 12%.
- k_{RF} = 7%.
- Tax rate = 40%.
- $beta_{Division}$ = 1.7.
- Market risk premium = 6%.

- Beta = 1.7, so division has more market risk than average.
- Division's required return on equity:

$$k_s = k_{RF} + (k_M - k_{RF})b_{Div.}$$
$$= 7\% + (6\%)1.7 = 17.2\%.$$

$$WACC_{Div.} = w_d k_d(1 - T) + w_c k_s$$
$$= 0.4(12\%)(0.6) + 0.6(17.2\%)$$
$$= 13.2\%.$$

How does the division's market risk compare with the firm's overall market risk?

- Division WACC = 13.2% versus company WACC = 11.1%.
- Indicates that the division's market risk is greater than firm's average project.
- "Typical" projects within this division would be accepted if their returns are above 13.2%.

EXAM-TYPE PROBLEMS

10-1. Barak Company's 8 percent coupon rate, quarterly payment, $1,000 par value bond, which matures in 20 years, currently sells at a price of $686.86. The company's tax rate is 40 percent. Based on the nominal interest rate, not the EAR, what is the firm's component cost of debt for purposes of calculating the WACC? (7.32%)

10-2. Allison Engines Corporation has established a target capital structure of 40 percent debt and 60 percent common equity. The current market price of the firm's stock is P_0 = $28; its last dividend was D_0 = $2.20, and its expected dividend growth rate is 6 percent. Allison can issue new common stock at a flotation cost of 15 percent. What is Allison's marginal cost of outside equity capital, k_e? (15.8%)

10-3. Gator Services Unlimited's (GSU) financial analyst must determine the firm's WACC for use in capital budgeting. She has gathered the following relevant data:

(1) Target capital structure: Debt 55 percent, Common equity 45 percent.

(2) Interest rate on new debt = 10%.

(3) GSU's current stock price = $42.50; its last dividend was $3.00.

(4) The firm's constant growth rate is 10 percent; its tax rate is 35 percent.

What is GSU's WACC? (11.57%)

10-4. The Hiers Company has a target capital structure of 42 percent debt and 58 percent equity. The yield to maturity on the company's bonds is 11 percent, and the company's tax rate is 40 percent. Hiers' treasurer has calculated the company's WACC as 10.53 percent. What is the company's cost of equity capital, according to the treasurer's calculation? (13.38%)

11-26 Assume that you recently went to work for Allied Components Company, a supplier of auto repair parts used in the after-market with products from DaimlerChrysler, Ford, and other auto makers. Your boss, the chief financial officer (CFO), has just handed you the estimated cash flows for two proposed projects. Project L involves adding a new item to the firm's ignition system line; it would take some time to build up the market for this product, so the cash inflows would increase over time. Project S involves an add-on to an existing line, and its cash flows would decrease over time. Both projects have 3-year lives, because Allied is planning to introduce entirely new models after 3 years.

Here are the projects' net cash flows (in thousands of dollars):

	Expected Net Cash Flow	
Year	Project L	Project S
0	($100)	($100)
1	10	70
2	60	50
3	80	20

Depreciation, salvage values, net operating working capital requirements, and tax effects are all included in these cash flows.

The CFO also made subjective risk assessments of each project, and he concluded that both projects have risk characteristics that are similar to the firm's average project. Allied's weighted average cost of capital is 10 percent. You must now determine whether one or both of the projects should be accepted.

a. What is capital budgeting? Are there any similarities between a firm's capital budgeting decisions and an individual's investment decisions?

b. What is the difference between independent and mutually exclusive projects? Between projects with normal and nonnormal cash flows?

c. (1) What is the payback period? Find the paybacks for Projects L and S.

(2) What is the rationale for the payback method? According to the payback criterion, which project or projects should be accepted if the firm's maximum acceptable payback is 2 years, and if Projects L and S are independent? If they are mutually exclusive?

(3) What is the difference between the regular and discounted payback periods?

(4) What is the main disadvantage of discounted payback? Is the payback method of any real usefulness in capital budgeting decisions?

d. (1) Define the term *net present value (NPV)*. What is each project's NPV?

(2) What is the rationale behind the NPV method? According to NPV, which project or projects should be accepted if they are independent? Mutually exclusive?

(3) Would the NPVs change if the cost of capital changed?

e. (1) Define the term *internal rate of return (IRR)*. What is each project's IRR?

(2) How is the IRR on a project related to the YTM on a bond?

(3) What is the logic behind the IRR method? According to IRR, which projects should be accepted if they are independent? Mutually exclusive?

(4) Would the projects' IRRs change if the cost of capital changed?

f. (1) Draw NPV profiles for Projects L and S. At what discount rate do the profiles cross?

(2) Look at your NPV profile graph without referring to the actual NPVs and IRRs. Which project or projects should be accepted if they are independent? Mutually exclusive? Explain. Are your answers correct at any cost of capital less than 23.6 percent?

g. (1) What is the underlying cause of ranking conflicts between NPV and IRR?

(2) What is the "reinvestment rate assumption," and how does it affect the NPV versus IRR conflict?

(3) Which method is the best? Why?

h. (1) Define the term *modified IRR (MIRR)*. Find the MIRRs for Projects L and S.

(2) What are the MIRR's advantages and disadvantages vis-à-vis the regular IRR? What are the MIRR's advantages and disadvantages vis-à-vis the NPV?

i. As a separate project (Project P), the firm is considering sponsoring a pavilion at the upcoming World's Fair. The pavilion would cost $800,000, and it is expected to result in $5 million of incremental cash inflows during its 1 year of operation. However, it would then take another year, and $5 million of costs, to demolish the site and return it to its original condition. Thus, Project P's expected net cash flows look like this (in millions of dollars):

Year	Net Cash Flows
0	($0.8)
1	5.0
2	(5.0)

The project is estimated to be of average risk, so its cost of capital is 10 percent.

(1) What is Project P's NPV? What is its IRR? Its MIRR?

(2) Draw Project P's NPV profile. Does Project P have normal or nonnormal cash flows? Should this project be accepted?

CHAPTER 11
The Basics of Capital Budgeting

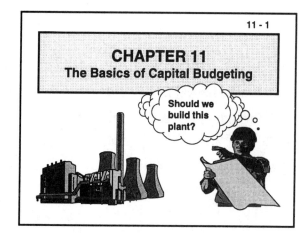

Should we build this plant?

What is capital budgeting?

- Analysis of potential additions to fixed assets.
- Long-term decisions; involve large expenditures.
- Very important to firm's future.

Steps

1. Estimate CFs (inflows & outflows).
2. Assess riskiness of CFs.
3. Determine k = WACC (adj.).
4. Find NPV and/or IRR.
5. Accept if NPV > 0 and/or IRR > WACC.

What is the difference between independent and mutually exclusive projects?

Projects are:

> independent, if the cash flows of one are unaffected by the acceptance of the other.

> mutually exclusive, if the cash flows of one can be adversely impacted by the acceptance of the other.

An Example of Mutually Exclusive Projects

BRIDGE vs. **BOAT** to get products across a river.

Normal Cash Flow Project

> Cost (negative CF) followed by a series of positive cash inflows. <u>One</u> change of signs.

Nonnormal Cash Flow Project

> <u>Two</u> or more changes of signs. Most common: Cost (negative CF), then string of positive CFs, then cost to close project. Nuclear power plant, strip mine.

Inflow (+) or Outflow (-) in Year

0	1	2	3	4	5	N	NN
-	+	+	+	+	+	N	
-	+	+	+	+	-		NN
-	-	-	+	+	+	N	
+	+	+	-	-	-	N	
-	+	+	-	+	-		NN

What is the payback period?

The number of years required to recover a project's cost,

or how long does it take to get our money back?

Payback for Project L
(Long: Large CFs in later years)

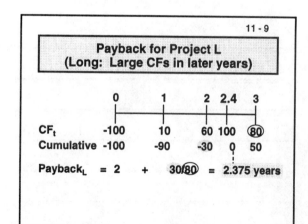

	0	1	2	2.4	3
CF_t	-100	10	60	100	(80)
Cumulative	-100	-90	-30	0	50

$Payback_L = 2 + 30/(80) = 2.375$ years

Project S (Short: CFs come quickly)

	0	1	1.6	2	3
CF_t	-100	70	100	50	20
Cumulative	-100	-30	0	20	40

$Payback_L = 1 + 30/50 = 1.6$ years

Strengths of Payback

1. Provides an indication of a project's risk and liquidity.
2. Easy to calculate and understand.

Weaknesses of Payback

1. Ignores the TVM.
2. Ignores CFs occurring after the payback period.

Discounted Payback: Uses discounted rather than raw CFs.

	0	10%	1	2	3
CF_t	-100		10	60	80
$PVCF_t$	-100		9.09	49.59	60.11
Cumulative	-100		-90.91	-41.32	18.79

Discounted payback $= 2 + 41.32/60.11 = 2.7$ years

Recover invest. + cap. costs in 2.7 years.

NPV: Sum of the PVs of inflows and outflows.

$$NPV = \sum_{t=0}^{n} \frac{CF_t}{(1+k)^t}.$$

What is Project L's NPV?

Project L:

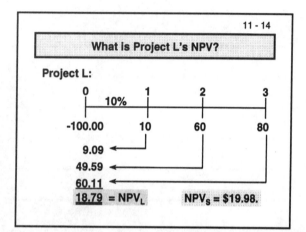

```
        0           1           2           3
        |———10%———|———————|———————|
    -100.00        10          60          80
       9.09   ◄———————
      49.59   ◄———————————————
      60.11   ◄———————————————————————
     18.79  = NPV_L        NPV_S = $19.98.
```

Calculator Solution

Enter in CFLO for L:

-100   CF₀
  10   CF₁
  60   CF₂
  80   CF₃
  10   I   NPV = 18.78 = NPV_L

Rationale for the NPV Method

NPV = PV inflows − Cost
= Net gain in wealth.

Accept project if NPV > 0.

Choose between mutually exclusive projects on basis of higher NPV. Adds most value.

Using NPV method, which project(s) should be accepted?

- If Projects S and L are mutually exclusive, accept S because $NPV_s > NPV_L$.

- If S & L are independent, accept both; NPV > 0.

Internal Rate of Return: IRR

```
   0        1        2        3
   |        |        |        |
  CF₀      CF₁      CF₂      CF₃
  Cost       ←— Inflows —→
```

IRR is the discount rate that forces PV inflows = cost. This is the same as forcing NPV = 0.

NPV: Enter k, solve for NPV.

$$\sum_{t=0}^{n} \frac{CF_t}{(1+k)^t} = NPV.$$

IRR: Enter NPV = 0, solve for IRR.

$$\sum_{t=0}^{n} \frac{CF_t}{(1+IRR)^t} = 0.$$

_____
_____
_____
_____
_____
_____
_____

What's Project L's IRR?

Enter CFs in CFLO, then press IRR:
IRR$_L$ = 18.13%. IRR$_S$ = 23.56%.

_____
_____
_____
_____
_____
_____
_____

Find IRR if CFs are constant:

Or, with CFLO, enter CFs and press
IRR = 9.70%.

_____
_____
_____
_____
_____
_____
_____

Q. How is a project's IRR related to a bond's YTM?

A. They are the same thing. A bond's YTM is the IRR if you invest in the bond.

IRR = 7.08% (use TVM or CFLO).

Rationale for the IRR Method

If IRR > WACC, then the project's rate of return is greater than its cost--some return is left over to boost stockholders' returns.

Example: WACC = 10%, IRR = 15%. Profitable.

IRR Acceptance Criteria

■ If IRR > k, accept project.

■ If IRR < k, reject project.

Decisions on Projects S and L per IRR

- If S and L are independent, accept both. IRRs > k = 10%.

- If S and L are mutually exclusive, accept S because $IRR_S > IRR_L$.

Construct NPV Profiles

Enter CFs in CFLO and find NPV_L and NPV_S at different discount rates:

k	NPV_L	NPV_S
0	50	40
5	33	29
10	19	20
15	7	12
20	(4)	5

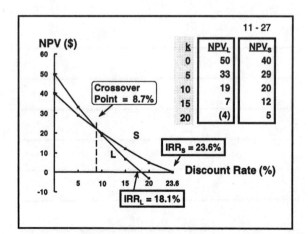

k	NPV_L	NPV_S
0	50	40
5	33	29
10	19	20
15	7	12
20	(4)	5

Crossover Point = 8.7%

$IRR_S = 23.6\%$

$IRR_L = 18.1\%$

NPV and IRR always lead to the same accept/reject decision for independent projects:

Mutually Exclusive Projects

$k < 8.7: NPV_L > NPV_S, IRR_S > IRR_L$
CONFLICT
$k > 8.7: NPV_S > NPV_L, IRR_S > IRR_L$
NO CONFLICT

To Find the Crossover Rate

1. Find cash flow differences between the projects. See data at beginning of the case.
2. Enter these differences in CFLO register, then press IRR. Crossover rate = 8.68%, rounded to 8.7%.
3. Can subtract S from L or vice versa, but better to have first CF negative.
4. If profiles don't cross, one project dominates the other.

Two Reasons NPV Profiles Cross

1. **Size (scale) differences.** Smaller project frees up funds at t = 0 for investment. The higher the opportunity cost, the more valuable these funds, so high k favors small projects.

2. **Timing differences.** Project with faster payback provides more CF in early years for reinvestment. If k is high, early CF especially good, $NPV_S > NPV_L$.

Reinvestment Rate Assumptions

- NPV assumes reinvest at k (opportunity cost of capital).

- IRR assumes reinvest at IRR.

- Reinvest at opportunity cost, k, is more realistic, so NPV method is best. NPV should be used to choose between mutually exclusive projects.

Managers like rates--prefer IRR to NPV comparisons. Can we give them a better IRR?

Yes, MIRR is the discount rate that causes the PV of a project's terminal value (TV) to equal the PV of costs. TV is found by compounding inflows at WACC.

Thus, MIRR assumes cash inflows are reinvested at WACC.

MIRR for Project L (k = 10%)

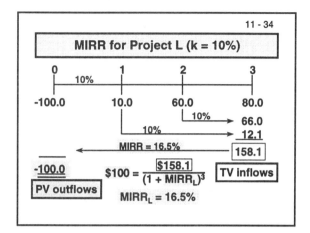

$$\$100 = \frac{\$158.1}{(1 + MIRR_L)^3}$$

PV outflows

TV inflows

$MIRR_L = 16.5\%$

To find TV with HP 10B, enter in CFLO:

$CF_0 = 0$, $CF_1 = 10$, $CF_2 = 60$, $CF_3 = 80$

$I = 10$

NPV = 118.78 = PV of inflows.

Enter PV = -118.78, N = 3, I = 10, PMT = 0.
Press FV = 158.10 = FV of inflows.

Enter FV = 158.10, PV = -100, PMT = 0,
N = 3.
Press I = 16.50% = MIRR.

Why use MIRR versus IRR?

MIRR correctly assumes reinvestment at opportunity cost = WACC. MIRR also avoids the problem of multiple IRRs.

Managers like rate of return comparisons, and MIRR is better for this than IRR.

Pavilion Project: NPV and IRR?

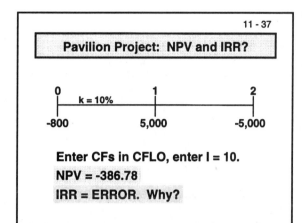

0		1		2
k = 10%				
-800		5,000		-5,000

Enter CFs in CFLO, enter I = 10.
NPV = -386.78
IRR = ERROR. Why?

We got IRR = ERROR because there
are 2 IRRs. Nonnormal CFs--two sign
changes. Here's a picture:

NPV Profile

NPV

450

$IRR_2 = 400\%$

0   100   400   k

$IRR_1 = 25\%$

-800

Logic of Multiple IRRs

1. At very low discount rates, the PV of
   CF_2 is large & negative, so NPV < 0.

2. At very high discount rates, the PV of
   both CF_1 and CF_2 are low, so CF_0
   dominates and again NPV < 0.

3. In between, the discount rate hits CF_2
   harder than CF_1, so NPV > 0.

4. **Result: 2 IRRs.**

Could find IRR with calculator:

1. **Enter CFs as before.**
2. **Enter a "guess" as to IRR by storing the guess. Try 10%:**

   10 ▇▇ STO

   ▇▇ IRR = 25% = lower IRR

   Now guess large IRR, say, 200:

   200 ▇▇ STO

   ▇▇ IRR = 400% = upper IRR

When there are nonnormal CFs and more than one IRR, use MIRR:

```
0               1               2
|---------------|---------------|
-800,000    5,000,000      -5,000,000
```

PV outflows @ 10% = -4,932,231.40.
TV inflows @ 10% = 5,500,000.00.
MIRR = 5.6%

Accept Project P?

NO. Reject because MIRR = 5.6% < k = 10%.

Also, if MIRR < k, NPV will be negative: NPV = -$386,777.

EXAM-TYPE PROBLEMS

11-1. A company is analyzing two mutually exclusive projects, S and L, whose cash flows are shown below:

Years 0		1	2	3	4
	12%				
S -1,100		900	350	50	10
L -1,100		0	300	500	850

The company's cost of capital is 12 percent, and it can get an unlimited amount of capital at that cost. What is the *regular IRR* (not MIRR) of the *better* project? (Hint: Note that the better project may or may not be the one with the higher IRR.) (13.09%)

11-2. As the director of capital budgeting for Lasser Company, you are evaluating two mutually exclusive projects with the following net cash flows:

Year	Project X	Project Z
0	-$100	-$100
1	50	10
2	40	30
3	30	40
4	10	60

Do the two NPV profiles cross in the relevant part of the NPV profile graph (the upper right quadrant) and, if they do cross, at what rate do the profiles cross? (7.17%)

11-3. Below are the returns of Nulook Cosmetics and the "market" over a 3-year period:

Year	Nulook	Market
1	9%	6%
2	15	10
3	36	24

Nulook finances internally using only retained earnings, and it uses the Capital Asset Pricing Model with a historical beta to determine its cost of equity. Currently, the risk-free rate is 7 percent, and the estimated market risk premium is 6 percent. Nulook is evaluating a project that has a cost today of $2,028 and will provide estimated after-tax cash inflows of $1,000 at the end of each of the next 3 years. What is this project's MIRR? (20.01%)

12-19 After seeing Snapple's success with noncola soft drinks and learning of Coke's and Pepsi's interest, Allied Food Products has decided to consider an expansion of its own in the fruit juice business. The product being considered is fresh lemon juice. Assume that you were recently hired as assistant to the director of capital budgeting, and you must evaluate the new project.

The lemon juice would be produced in an unused building adjacent to Allied's Fort Myers plant; Allied owns the building, which is fully depreciated. The required equipment would cost $200,000, plus an additional $40,000 for shipping and installation. In addition, inventories would rise by $25,000, while accounts payable would go up by $5,000. All of these costs would be incurred at t = 0. By a special ruling, the machinery could be depreciated under the MACRS system as 3-year property.

The project is expected to operate for 4 years, at which time it will be terminated. The cash inflows are assumed to begin 1 year after the project is undertaken, or at t = 1, and to continue out to t = 4. At the end of the project's life (t = 4), the equipment is expected to have a salvage value of $25,000.

Unit sales are expected to total 100,000 cans per year, and the expected sales price is $2.00 per can. Cash operating costs for the project (total operating costs less depreciation) are expected to total 60 percent of dollar sales. Allied's tax rate is 40 percent, and its weighted average cost of capital is 10 percent. Tentatively, the lemon juice project is assumed to be of equal risk to Allied's other assets.

You have been asked to evaluate the project and to make a recommendation as to whether it should be accepted or rejected. To guide you in your analysis, your boss gave you the following set of questions.

a. Draw a time line that shows when the net cash inflows and outflows will occur, and explain how the time line can be used to help structure the analysis.

b. Allied has a standard form that is used in the capital budgeting process; see Table IC12-1. Part of the table has been completed, but you must replace the blanks with the missing numbers.

Table IC12-1. Allied's Lemon Juice Project
(Total Cost in Thousands)

End of Year:	0	1	2	3	4
I. Investment Outlay					
Equipment cost					
Installation					
Increase in inventory					
Increase in accounts payable	___				
Total net investment	≡≡				
II. Operating Cash Flows					
Unit sales (thousands)			100		
Price/unit		$ 2.00	$ 2.00	___	___
Total revenues					$200.0
Operating costs, excluding depreciation			$120.0		
Depreciation				36.0	16.8
Total costs		$199.2	$228.0	___	___
Oper. income bef. taxes				$44.0	
Taxes on oper. income		0.3	___		25.3
Oper. income after taxes				$26.4	
Depreciation	___	79.2		36.0	___
Operating cash flow	$ 0.0	$ 79.7			$ 54.7
III. Terminal Year Cash Flows					
Return of net operating working capital					
Salvage value					
Tax on salvage value					
Total termination cash flows					___
IV. Net Cash Flows					
Net cash flow	($260.0)	___	___	___	$ 89.7
V. Results					
NPV =					
IRR =					
MIRR =					
Payback =					

Complete the table in the following steps:

(1) Fill in the blanks under Year 0 for the initial investment outlay.

(2) Complete the table for unit sales, sales price, total revenues, and operating costs excluding depreciation.

(3) Complete the depreciation data.

(4) Now complete the table down to operating income after taxes, and then down to net cash flows.

(5) Now fill in the blanks under Year 4 for the terminal cash flows, and complete the net cash flow line. Discuss net operating working capital. What would have happened if the machinery were sold for less than its book value?

c. (1) Allied uses debt in its capital structure, so some of the money used to finance the project will be debt. Given this fact, should the projected cash flows be revised to show projected interest charges? Explain.

(2) Suppose you learned that Allied had spent $50,000 to renovate the building last year, expensing these costs. Should this cost be reflected in the analysis? Explain.

(3) Now suppose you learned that Allied could lease its building to another party and earn $25,000 per year. Should that fact be reflected in the analysis? If so, how?

(4) Now assume that the lemon juice project would take away profitable sales from Allied's fresh orange juice business. Should that fact be reflected in your analysis? If so, how?

d. Disregard all the assumptions made in part c, and assume there was no alternative use for the building over the next 4 years. Now calculate the project's NPV, IRR, MIRR, and regular payback. Do these indicators suggest that the project should be accepted?

e. If this project had been a replacement rather than an expansion project, how would the analysis have changed? Think about the changes that would have to occur in the cash flow table.

f. Assume that inflation is expected to average 5 percent over the next 4 years; that this expectation is reflected in the WACC; and that inflation will increase variable costs and revenues by the same percentage, 5 percent. Does it appear that inflation has been dealt with properly in the analysis? If not, what should be done, and how would the required adjustment affect the decision? You can modify the numbers in the table to quantify your results.

Although inflation was considered in the initial analysis, the riskiness of the project was not considered. The expected cash flows, considering inflation (in thousands of dollars), are given in Table IC12-2. Allied's overall cost of capital (WACC) is 10 percent.

Table IC12-2. Allied's Lemon Juice Project Considering Inflation
(in Thousands)

	Year				
	0	1	2	3	4
Investment in:					
Fixed assets	($240)				
Net operating					
working capital	(20)				
Unit sales (thousands)		100	100	100	100
Sale price (dollars)		$2.100	$2.205	$2.315	$2.431
Total revenues		$210.0	$220.5	$231.5	$243.1
Cash operating costs (60%)		126.0	132.3	138.9	145.9
Depreciation		79.2	108.0	36.0	16.8
Operating income before taxes		$ 4.8	($ 19.8)	$ 56.6	$ 80.4
Taxes on operating income (40%)		1.9	(7.9)	22.6	32.1
Operating income after taxes		$ 2.9	($ 11.9)	$ 34.0	$ 48.3
Plus depreciation		79.2	108.0	36.0	16.8
Operating cash flow		$ 82.1	$ 96.1	$ 70.0	$ 65.1
Salvage value					25.0
Tax on SV (40%)					(10.0)
Recovery of NOWC					20.0
Net cash flow	($260)	$ 82.1	$ 96.1	$ 70.0	$100.1
Cumulative cash flows					
for payback:	(260.0)	(177.9)	(81.8)	(11.8)	88.3
Compounded inflows					
for MIRR:		109.2	116.3	77.0	100.1
Terminal value of inflows:					402.6

NPV at 10% cost of capital = $15.0
IRR   = 12.6%
MIRR   = 11.6%

You have been asked to answer the following questions.

g. (1) What are the three levels, or types, of project risk that are normally considered?

   (2) Which type is most relevant?

   (3) Which type is easiest to measure?

   (4) Are the three types of risk generally highly correlated?

h. (1) What is sensitivity analysis?

(2) Discuss how one would perform a sensitivity analysis on the unit sales, salvage value, and cost of capital for the project. Assume that each of these variables deviates from its base-case, or expected, value by plus and minus 10, 20, and 30 percent. Explain how you would calculate the NPV, IRR, MIRR, and payback for each case.

(3) What is the primary weakness of sensitivity analysis? What are its primary advantages?

i. Assume that you are confident about the estimates of all the variables that affect the cash flows except unit sales. If product acceptance is poor, sales would be only 75,000 units a year, while a strong consumer response would produce sales of 125,000 units. In either case, cash costs would still amount to 60 percent of revenues. You believe that there is a 25 percent chance of poor acceptance, a 25 percent chance of excellent acceptance, and a 50 percent chance of average acceptance (the base case).

(1) What is the worst-case NPV? The best-case NPV?

(2) Use the worst-, most likely (or base), and best-case NPVs, with their probabilities of occurrence, to find the project's expected NPV, standard deviation, and coefficient of variation.

j. (1) Assume that Allied's average project has a coefficient of variation (CV) in the range of 1.25 to 1.75. Would the lemon juice project be classified as high risk, average risk, or low risk? What type of risk is being measured here?

(2) Based on common sense, how highly correlated do you think the project would be with the firm's other assets? (Give a correlation coefficient or range of coefficients, based on your judgment.)

(3) How would this correlation coefficient and the previously calculated σ combine to affect the project's contribution to corporate, or within-firm, risk? Explain.

k. (1) Based on your judgment, what do you think the project's correlation coefficient would be with respect to the general economy and thus with returns on "the market"?

(2) How would correlation with the economy affect the project's market risk?

l. (1) Allied typically adds or subtracts 3 percentage points to the overall cost of capital to adjust for risk. Should the lemon juice project be accepted?

(2) What subjective risk factors should be considered before the final decision is made?

m. In recent months, Allied's group has begun to focus on real option analysis.

    (1) What is real option analysis?

    (2) What are some examples of projects with embedded real options?

CHAPTER 12
Cash Flow Estimation and Risk Analysis

- Relevant cash flows
- Incorporating inflation
- Types of risk
- Risk analysis
- Real options

Proposed Project

- Cost: $200,000 + $10,000 shipping + $30,000 installation. Depreciable cost: $240,000.
- Inventories will rise by $25,000 and payables by $5,000.
- Economic life = 4 years.
- Salvage value = $25,000.
- MACRS 3-year class.

- Sales: 100,000 units/year @ $2.
- Variable cost = 60% of sales.
- Tax rate = 40%.
- WACC = 10%.

Set up, without numbers, a time line for the project's cash flows.

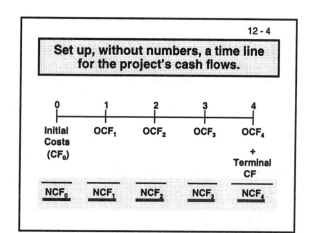

Investment at t = 0:

Equipment	-$200
Installation & Shipping	-40
Increase in inventories	-25
Increase in A/P	5
Net CF_0	-$260

$$\Delta NOWC = \$25 - \$5 = \$20.$$

What's the annual depreciation?

Year	Rate	x	Basis	Depreciation
1	0.33		$240	$ 79
2	0.45		240	108
3	0.15		240	36
4	0.07		240	17
	1.00			$240

Due to 1/2-year convention, a 3-year asset is depreciated over 4 years.

Operating cash flows:

	1	2	3	4
Revenues	200	200	200	200
Op. Cost, 60%	-120	-120	-120	-120
Depreciation	-79	-108	-36	-17
Oper. inc. (BT)	1	-28	44	63
Tax, 40%	--	-11	18	25
Oper. inc. (AT)	1	-17	26	38
Add. Depr'n	79	108	36	17
Op. CF	80	91	62	55

Net Terminal CF at t = 4:

Recovery of NOWC	$20
Salvage Value	25
Tax on SV (40%)	-10
Net termination CF	$35

Q. Always a tax on SV? Ever a positive tax number?

Q. How is NOWC recovered?

Should CFs include interest expense? Dividends?

■ No. The cost of capital is accounted for by discounting at the 10% WACC, so deducting interest and dividends would be "double counting" financing costs.

Suppose $50,000 had been spent last year to improve the building. Should this cost be included in the analysis?

No. This is a sunk cost.
Analyze incremental investment.

Suppose the plant could be leased out for $25,000 a year. Would this affect the analysis?

■ Yes. Accepting the project means foregoing the $25,000. This is an opportunity cost, and it should be charged to the project.

■ A.T. opportunity cost = $25,000(1 – T) = $25,000(0.6) = $15,000 annual cost.

If the new product line would decrease sales of the firm's other lines, would this affect the analysis?

■ Yes. The effect on other projects' CFs is an "externality."

■ Net CF loss per year on other lines would be a cost to this project.

■ Externalities can be positive or negative, i.e., complements or substitutes.

Here are all the project's net CFs (in thousands) on a time line:

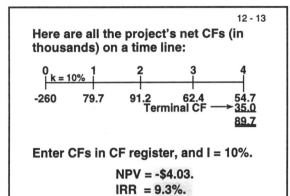

Enter CFs in CF register, and I = 10%.

NPV = -$4.03.
IRR = 9.3%.

What's the project's MIRR?

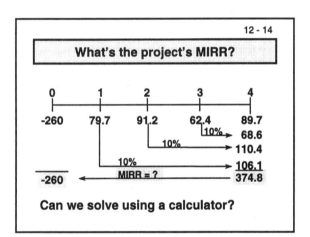

Can we solve using a calculator?

Yes.

$CF_0 = 0$
$CF_1 = 79.7$
$CF_2 = 91.2$
$CF_3 = 62.4$
$CF_4 = 89.7$
$I = 10$
■ NPV = 255.97

Use the FV = TV of inputs to find MIRR

INPUTS	4		-260	0	374.8
	N	I/YR	PV	PMT	FV
OUTPUT		9.6			

MIRR = 9.6%. Since MIRR < k = 10%, reject the project.

What's the payback period?

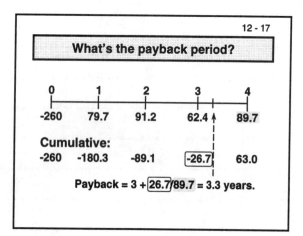

0	1	2	3	4
-260	79.7	91.2	62.4	89.7

Cumulative:

-260	-180.3	-89.1	-26.7	63.0

Payback = 3 + 26.7/89.7 = 3.3 years.

If this were a replacement rather than a new project, would the analysis change?

Yes. The old equipment would be sold, and the incremental CFs would be the changes from the old to the new situation.

■ The relevant depreciation would be the change with the new equipment.

■ Also, if the firm sold the old machine now, it would not receive the SV at the end of the machine's life. This is an opportunity cost for the replacement project.

Q. If E(INFL) = 5%, is NPV biased?

A. YES. $NPV = \sum_{t=0}^{n} \dfrac{CF_t}{(1+k)^t} = \dfrac{Rev_t - Cost_t}{(1+k)^t}$.

$k = k^* + IP + DRP + LP + MRP$.

Inflation is in denominator but not in numerator, so downward bias to NPV. Should build inflation into CF forecasts.

Consider project with 5% inflation. Investment remains same, $260. Terminal CF remains same, $35.

Operating cash flows:

	1	2	3	4
Revenues	210	220	232	243
Op. cost 60%	-126	-132	-139	-146
Depr'n	-79	-108	-36	-17
Oper. inc. (BT)	5	-20	57	80
Tax, 40%	2	-8	23	32
Oper. inc. (AT)	3	-12	34	48
Add Depr'n	79	108	36	17
Op. CF	82	96	70	65

Here are all the project's net CFs (in thousands) when inflation is considered.

```
   0   k = 10%  1         2         3         4
   ├──────────┼─────────┼─────────┼─────────┤
  -260       82.1      96.1      70.0      65.1
                      Terminal CF ───────►  35.0
                                           100.1
```

Enter CFs in CF register, and I = 10%.

NPV = $15.0. Project should be accepted.
IRR = 12.6%.

What are the 3 types of project risk?

- Stand-alone risk
- Corporate risk
- Market risk

What is stand-alone risk?

- The project's total risk if it were operated independently.
- Usually measured by standard deviation (or coefficient of variation).
- However, it ignores the firm's diversification among projects and investor's diversification among firms.

What is corporate risk?

- The project's risk giving consideration to the firm's other projects, i.e., diversification within the firm.

- Corporate risk is a function of the project's NPV and standard deviation and its correlation with the returns on other projects in the firm.

What is market risk?

- The project's risk to a well-diversified investor.

- Theoretically, it is measured by the project's beta and it considers both corporate and stockholder diversification.

Which type of risk is most relevant?

- Market risk is the most relevant risk for capital projects, because management's primary goal is shareholder wealth maximization.

- However, since total risk affects creditors, customers, suppliers, and employees, it should not be completely ignored.

12 - 28

Which risk is the easiest to measure?

- Stand-alone risk is the easiest to measure. Firms often focus on stand-alone risk when making capital budgeting decisions.

- Focusing on stand-alone risk is not theoretically correct, but it does not necessarily lead to poor decisions.

---

12 - 29

Are the three types of risk generally highly correlated?

Yes. Since most projects the firm undertakes are in its core business, stand-alone risk is likely to be highly correlated with its corporate risk, which in turn is likely to be highly correlated with its market risk.

---

12 - 30

What is sensitivity analysis?

- Sensitivity analysis measures the effect of changes in a variable on the project's NPV.

- To perform a sensitivity analysis, all variables are fixed at their expected values, except for the variable in question which is allowed to fluctuate.

- Resulting changes in NPV are noted.

What are the primary advantages and disadvantages of sensitivity analysis?

ADVANTAGE:

Sensitivity analysis identifies variables that may have the greatest potential impact on profitability. This allows management to focus on those variables that are most important.

DISADVANTAGES:

Sensitivity analysis does not reflect the effects of diversification.

Sensitivity analysis does not incorporate any information about the possible magnitudes of the forecast errors.

Perform a scenario analysis of the project, based on changes in the sales forecast.

Assume that we are confident of all the variables that affect the cash flows, except unit sales. We expect unit sales to adhere to the following profile:

Case	Probability	Unit sales
Worst	0.25	75,000
Base	0.50	100,000
Best	0.25	125,000

If cash costs are to remain 60% of revenues, and all other factors are constant, we can solve for project NPV under each scenario.

Case	Probability	NPV
Worst	0.25	($27.8)
Base	0.50	$15.0
Best	0.25	$57.8

Use these scenarios, with their given probabilities, to find the project's expected NPV, σ_{NPV}, and CV_{NPV}.

$E(NPV) = .25(-\$27.8) + .5(\$15.0) + .25(\$57.8)$

$E(NPV) =$ $15.0.

$\sigma_{NPV} = [.25(-\$27.8-\$15.0)^2 + .5(\$15.0-\$15.0)^2 + .25(\$57.8-\$15.0)^2]^{1/2}$

$\sigma_{NPV} =$ $30.3.

$CV_{NPV} =$ $30.3 / $15.0 = 2.0.

The firm's average projects have coefficients of variation ranging from 1.25 to 1.75. Would this project be of high, average, or low risk?

The project's CV of 2.0 would suggest that it would be classified as high risk.

Is this project likely to be correlated with the firm's business? How would it contribute to the firm's overall risk?

- We would expect a positive correlation with the firm's aggregate cash flows.

- As long as correlation is not perfectly positive (i.e., $r \neq 1$), we would expect it to contribute to the lowering of the firm's total risk.

If the project had a high correlation with the economy, how would corporate and market risk be affected?

The project's corporate risk would not be directly affected. However, when combined with the project's high stand-alone risk, correlation with the economy would suggest that market risk (beta) is high.

If the firm uses a +/-3% risk adjustment for the cost of capital, should the project be accepted?

- Reevaluating this project at a 13% cost of capital (due to high stand-alone risk), the NPV of the project is -$2.2 .

- If, however, it were a low-risk project, we would use a 7% cost of capital and the project NPV is $34.1.

What subjective risk factors should be considered before a decision is made?

- Numerical analysis sometimes fails to capture all sources of risk for a project.

- If the project has the potential for a lawsuit, it is more risky than previously thought.

- If assets can be redeployed or sold easily, the project may be less risky.

What is real option analysis?

- Real options exist when managers can influence the size and riskiness of a project's cash flows by taking different actions during the project's life.

- Real option analysis incorporates typical NPV budgeting analysis with an analysis for opportunities resulting from managers' decisions.

What are some examples of real options?

- Investment timing options
- Abandonment/shutdown options
- Growth/expansion options
- Flexibility options

EXAM-TYPE PROBLEMS

12-1. General Communications encounters significant uncertainty in its sales volume and price with its primary product. The firm uses scenario analysis to determine an expected NPV, which it then uses in its capital budget. The base-case, best-case, and worst-case scenarios and probabilities are provided in the following table. What are this product's expected NPV, standard deviation, and coefficient of variation? ($23,411,250; $19,682,424.70; 0.8407)

Scenario	Probability of Outcome	Unit Sales Volume	Sales Price	NPV (in 000's)
Worst case	0.20	9,000	$5,750	-$9,000
Base case	0.45	15,600	$7,000	+$20,500
Best case	0.35	21,500	$8,150	+$45,675

12-2. The Merry Milling Company is evaluating the proposed acquisition of a new milling machine. The machine's base price is $540,000, and it would cost another $62,500 to modify it for special use by your firm. The machine falls into the MACRS 3-year class, and it would be sold after 3 years for $325,000. (See Table 12A-2 for MACRS recovery allowance percentages.) The machine would require an increase in net operating working capital (inventory) of $27,500. The milling machine would have no effect on revenues, but it is expected to save the firm $220,000 per year in before-tax operating costs, mainly labor. The firm's marginal tax rate is 35 percent. If the project's cost of capital is 12 percent, should the machine be purchased? (Yes, NPV = $54,202)

12-3. The Metropolitan Oil Company is deciding whether to drill for oil on a tract of land that the company owns. The company estimates that the project would cost $13.6 million today. Metropolitan estimates that once drilled, the oil will generate positive net cash flows of $6.8 million a year at the end of each of the next 4 years. While the company is fairly confident about its cash flow forecast, it recognizes that if it waits 2 years, it would have more information about the local geology as well as the price of oil. Metropolitan estimates that if it waits 2 years, the project would cost $15.3 million. Moreover, if it waits 2 years, there is a 90 percent chance that the net cash flows would be $7.14 million a year for 4 years, and there is a 10 percent chance that the cash flows will be $3.74 million a year for 4 years. Assume that all cash flows are discounted at 10 percent.

a. If the company chooses to drill today, what is the project's net present value? ($7.9551 million)

b. Would it make sense to wait 2 years before deciding whether to drill? (No, NPV = $5.4542 million)

13-18 Assume that you have just been hired as business manager of Campus Deli (CD), which is located adjacent to the campus. Sales were $1,100,000 last year; variable costs were 60 percent of sales; and fixed costs were $40,000. Therefore, EBIT totaled $400,000. Because the university's enrollment is capped, EBIT is expected to be constant over time. Since no expansion capital is required, CD pays out all earnings as dividends. Assets are $2 million, and 80,000 shares are outstanding. The management group owns about 50 percent of the stock, which is traded in the over-the-counter market.

CD currently has no debt—it is an all-equity firm—and its 80,000 shares outstanding sell at a price of $25 per share, which is also the book value. The firm's federal-plus-state tax rate is 40 percent. On the basis of statements made in your finance text, you believe that CD's shareholders would be better off if some debt financing were used. When you suggested this to your new boss, she encouraged you to pursue the idea, but to provide support for the suggestion.

In today's market, the risk-free rate, k_{RF}, is 6 percent and the market risk premium, $k_M - k_{RF}$, is 6 percent. CD's unlevered beta, b_U, is 1.0. Since CD currently has no debt, its cost of equity (and WACC) is 12 percent.

If the firm were recapitalized, debt would be issued, and the borrowed funds would be used to repurchase stock. Stockholders, in turn, would use funds provided by the repurchase to buy equities in other fast-food companies similar to CD. You plan to complete your report by asking and then answering the following questions.

a. (1) What is business risk? What factors influence a firm's business risk?

   (2) What is operating leverage, and how does it affect a firm's business risk?

b. (1) What is meant by the terms "financial leverage" and "financial risk"?

   (2) How does financial risk differ from business risk?

c. Now, to develop an example that can be presented to CD's management as an illustration, consider two hypothetical firms, Firm U, with zero debt financing, and Firm L, with $10,000 of 12 percent debt. Both firms have $20,000 in total assets and a 40 percent federal-plus-state tax rate, and they have the following EBIT probability distribution for next year:

Probability	EBIT
0.25	$2,000
0.50	3,000
0.25	4,000

(1) Complete the partial income statements and the firms' ratios in Table IC13-1.

Table IC13-1. Income Statements and Ratios

	Firm U			Firm L		
Assets	$20,000	$20,000	$20,000	$20,000	$20,000	$20,000
Equity	$20,000	$20,000	$20,000	$10,000	$10,000	$10,000
Probability	0.25	0.50	0.25	0.25	0.50	0.25
Sales	$ 6,000	$ 9,000	$12,000	$ 6,000	$ 9,000	$12,000
Oper. costs	4,000	6,000	8,000	4,000	6,000	8,000
EBIT	$ 2,000	$ 3,000	$ 4,000	$ 2,000	$ 3,000	$ 4,000
Interest (12%)	0	0	0	1,200		1,200
EBT	$ 2,000	$ 3,000	$ 4,000	$ 800	$	$ 2,800
Taxes (40%)	800	1,200	1,600	320		1,120
Net income	$ 1,200	$ 1,800	$ 2,400	$ 480	$	$ 1,680
BEP	10.0%	15.0%	20.0%	10.0%	%	20.0%
ROE	6.0%	9.0%	12.0%	4.8%	%	16.8%
TIE	∞	∞	∞	1.7×	×	3.3×
E(BEP)		15.0%			%	
E(ROE)		9.0%			10.8%	
E(TIE)		∞			2.5×	
σ(BEP)		3.5%			%	
σ(ROE)		2.1%			4.2%	
σ(TIE)		0			0.6×	

(2) Be prepared to discuss each entry in the table and to explain how this example illustrates the impact of financial leverage on expected rate of return and risk.

d. After speaking with a local investment banker, you obtain the following estimates of the cost of debt at different debt levels (in thousands of dollars):

Amount Borrowed	Debt/Assets Ratio	Debt/Equity Ratio	Bond Rating	k_d
$ 0	0	0	--	--
250	0.125	0.1429	AA	8.0%
500	0.250	0.3333	A	9.0
750	0.375	0.6000	BBB	11.5
1,000	0.500	1.0000	BB	14.0

Now consider the optimal capital structure for CD.

(1) To begin, define the terms "optimal capital structure" and "target capital structure."

(2) Why does CD's bond rating and cost of debt depend on the amount of money borrowed?

(3) Assume that shares could be repurchased at the current market price of $25 per share. Calculate CD's expected EPS and TIE at debt levels of $0, $250,000, $500,000, $750,000, and $1,000,000. How many shares would remain after recapitalization under each scenario?

(4) Using the Hamada equation, what is the cost of equity if CD recapitalizes with $250,000 of debt? $500,000? $750,000? $1,000,000?

(5) Considering only the levels of debt discussed, what is the capital structure that minimizes CD's WACC?

(6) What would be the new stock price if CD recapitalizes with $250,000 of debt? $500,000? $750,000? $1,000,000? Recall that the payout ratio is 100 percent, so $g = 0$.

(7) Is EPS maximized at the debt level that maximizes share price? Why or why not?

(8) Considering only the levels of debt discussed, what is CD's optimal capital structure?

(9) What is the WACC at the optimal capital structure?

e. Suppose you discovered that CD had more business risk than you originally estimated. Describe how this would affect the analysis. What if the firm had less business risk than originally estimated?

f. What are some factors a manager should consider when establishing his or her firm's target capital structure?

g. Put labels on Figure IC13-1, and then discuss the graph as you might use it to explain to your boss why CD might want to use some debt.

Figure IC13-1
Relationship between Capital Structure and Stock Price

h. How does the existence of asymmetric information and signaling affect capital structure?

CHAPTER 13
Capital Structure and Leverage

- Business vs. financial risk
- Optimal capital structure
- Operating leverage
- Capital structure theory

What is business risk?

- Uncertainty about future operating income (EBIT), i.e., how well can we predict operating income?

- Note that business risk does not include financing effects.

Business risk is affected primarily by:

- Uncertainty about demand (sales).
- Uncertainty about output prices.
- Uncertainty about costs.
- Product, other types of liability.
- Operating leverage.

What is operating leverage, and how does it affect a firm's business risk?

- Operating leverage is the use of fixed costs rather than variable costs.

- If most costs are fixed, hence do not decline when demand falls, then the firm has high operating leverage.

- More operating leverage leads to more business risk, for then a small sales decline causes a big profit decline.

- What happens if variable costs change?

Typical situation: Can use operating leverage to get higher E(EBIT), but risk increases.

What is financial leverage? Financial risk?

- Financial leverage is the use of debt and preferred stock.
- Financial risk is the additional risk concentrated on common stockholders as a result of financial leverage.

Business Risk vs. Financial Risk

- Business risk depends on business factors such as competition, product liability, and operating leverage.
- Financial risk depends only on the types of securities issued: More debt, more financial risk. Concentrates business risk on stockholders.

Consider 2 Hypothetical Firms

Firm U	Firm L
No debt	$10,000 of 12% debt
$20,000 in assets	$20,000 in assets
40% tax rate	40% tax rate

Both firms have same operating leverage, business risk, and probability distribution of EBIT. Differ only with respect to use of debt (capital structure).

Firm U: Unleveraged

	Economy		
	Bad	**Avg.**	**Good**
Prob.	0.25	0.50	0.25
EBIT	$2,000	$3,000	$4,000
Interest	0	0	0
EBT	$2,000	$3,000	$4,000
Taxes (40%)	800	1,200	1,600
NI	$1,200	$1,800	$2,400

Firm L: Leveraged

	Economy		
	Bad	**Avg.**	**Good**
Prob.*	0.25	0.50	0.25
EBIT*	$2,000	$3,000	$4,000
Interest	1,200	1,200	1,200
EBT	$ 800	$1,800	$2,800
Taxes (40%)	320	720	1,120
NI	$ 480	$1,080	$1,680

*Same as for Firm U.

Firm U	Bad	Avg.	Good
BEP*	10.0%	15.0%	20.0%
ROE	6.0%	9.0%	12.0%
TIE	∞	∞	∞

Firm L	Bad	Avg.	Good
BEP*	10.0%	15.0%	20.0%
ROE	4.8%	10.8%	16.8%
TIE	1.67x	2.5x	3.3x

*BEP same for Firms U and L.

Expected Values:

	U	L
E(BEP)	15.0%	15.0%
E(ROE)	9.0%	10.8%
E(TIE)	∞	2.5x

Risk Measures:

	U	L
σ_{ROE}	2.12%	4.24%
CV_{ROE}	0.24	0.39

- For leverage to raise expected ROE, must have BEP > k_d.
- Why? If k_d > BEP, then the interest expense will be higher than the operating income produced by debt-financed assets, so leverage will depress income.

Conclusions

- Basic earning power = BEP = EBIT/Total assets is unaffected by financial leverage.
- L has higher expected ROE because BEP > k_d.
- L has much wider ROE (and EPS) swings because of fixed interest charges. Its higher expected return is accompanied by higher risk.

If debt increases, TIE falls.

$$TIE = \frac{EBIT}{Int}.$$

EBIT is constant (unaffected by use of debt), and since Int = k_dD, as D increases, TIE must fall.

Optimal Capital Structure

- That capital structure (mix of debt, preferred, and common equity) at which P_0 is maximized. Trades off higher E(ROE) and EPS against higher risk. The tax-related benefits of leverage are exactly offset by the debt's risk-related costs.
- The target capital structure is the mix of debt, preferred stock, and common equity with which the firm intends to raise capital.

Describe the sequence of events in a recapitalization.

- Campus Deli *announces* the recapitalization.
- New debt is *issued*.
- Proceeds are used to *repurchase* stock.

$$Shares\ bought = \frac{Debt\ issued}{Price\ per\ share}.$$

Cost of Debt at Different Debt Levels after Recapitalization

Amount borrowed	D/A ratio	D/E ratio	Bond rating	k_d
$ 0	0	0	--	--
250	0.125	0.1429	AA	8%
500	0.250	0.3333	A	9%
750	0.375	0.6000	BBB	11.5%
1,000	0.500	1.0000	BB	14%

Why does the bond rating and cost of debt depend upon the amount borrowed?

As the firm borrows more money, the firm increases its risk causing the firm's bond rating to decrease, and its cost of debt to increase.

What would the earnings per share be if Campus Deli recapitalized and used these amounts of debt: $0, $250,000, $500,000, $750,000? Assume EBIT = $400,000, T = 40%, and shares can be repurchased at $P_0 = 25.

D = 0:

$$EPS_0 = \frac{(EBIT - k_d D)(1 - T)}{\text{Shares outstanding}}$$

$$= \frac{(\$400,000)(0.6)}{80,000} = \$3.00.$$

$D = \$250$, $k_d = 8\%$.

$$\text{Shares repurchased} = \frac{\$250{,}000}{\$25} = 10{,}000.$$

$$EPS_1 = \frac{[\$400 - 0.08(\$250)](0.6)}{80 - 10}$$

$$= \$3.26.$$

$$TIE = \frac{EBIT}{I} = \frac{\$400}{\$20} = 20\times.$$

$D = \$500$, $k_d = 9\%$.

$$\text{Shares repurchased} = \frac{\$500}{\$25} = 20.$$

$$EPS_2 = \frac{[\$400 - 0.09(\$500)](0.6)}{80 - 20}$$

$$= \$3.55.$$

$$TIE = \frac{EBIT}{I} = \frac{\$400}{\$45} = 8.9\times.$$

$D = \$750$, $k_d = 11.5\%$.

$$\text{Shares repurchased} = \frac{\$750}{\$25} = 30.$$

$$EPS_3 = \frac{[\$400 - 0.115(\$750)](0.6)}{80 - 30}$$

$$= \$3.77.$$

$$TIE = \frac{EBIT}{I} = \frac{\$400}{\$86.25} = 4.6\times.$$

D = $1,000, k_d = 14%.

$$\text{Shares repurchased} = \frac{\$1,000}{\$25} = 40.$$

$$EPS_4 = \frac{[\$400 - 0.14(\$1,000)](0.6)}{80 - 40}$$

$$= \$3.90.$$

$$TIE = \frac{EBIT}{I} = \frac{\$400}{\$140} = 2.9\times.$$

Stock Price (Zero Growth)

$$P_0 = \frac{D_1}{k_s - g} = \frac{EPS}{k_s} = \frac{DPS}{k_s}.$$

If payout = 100%, then EPS = DPS and E(g) = 0.

We just calculated EPS = DPS. To find the expected stock price (P_0), we must find the appropriate k_s at each of the debt levels discussed.

What effect would increasing debt have on the cost of equity for the firm?

- If the level of debt increases, the riskiness of the firm increases.
- We have already observed the increase in the cost of debt.
- However, the riskiness of the firm's equity also increases, resulting in a higher k_s.

The Hamada Equation

- Because the increased use of debt causes both the costs of debt and equity to increase, we need to estimate the new cost of equity.
- The Hamada equation attempts to quantify the increased cost of equity due to financial leverage.
- Uses the unlevered beta of a firm, which represents the business risk of a firm as if it had no debt.

The Hamada Equation (cont'd)

$$b_L = b_U[1 + (1 - T)(D/E)].$$

The risk-free rate is 6%, as is the market risk premium. The unlevered beta of the firm is 1.0. We were previously told that total assets were $2,000,000.

Calculating Levered Betas

$D = \$250$ $k_s = k_{RF} + (k_M - k_{RF})b_L$

$b_L = b_U[1 + (1 - T)(D/E)]$
$b_L = 1.0[1 + (1 - 0.4)(\$250/\$1,750)]$
$b_L = 1.0[1 + (0.6)(0.1429)]$
$b_L = 1.0857.$

$k_s = k_{RF} + (k_M - k_{RF})b_L$
$k_s = 6.0\% + (6.0\%)1.0857 = 12.51\%.$

Table for Calculating Levered Betas

Amount borrowed	D/A ratio	D/E ratio	Levered Beta	k_s
$ 0	0.00%	0.00%	1.00	12.00%
250	12.50	14.29	1.09	12.51
500	25.00	33.33	1.20	13.20
750	37.50	60.00	1.36	14.16
1,000	50.00	100.00	1.60	15.60

Finding Optimal Capital Structure

■ The firm's optimal capital structure can be determined two ways:
 ● Minimizes WACC.
 ● Maximizes stock price.
■ Both methods yield the same results.

Minimizing the WACC

Amount borrowed	D/A ratio	E/A ratio	k_s	$k_d (1 - T)$	WACC
$ 0	0.00%	100.00%	12.00%	0.00%	12.00%
250	12.50	87.50	12.51	4.80	11.55
500	25.00	75.00	13.20	5.40	11.25
750	37.50	62.50	14.16	6.90	11.44
1,000	50.00	50.00	15.60	8.40	12.00

Maximizing Stock Price

Amount Borrowed	DPS	k_s	P_0
$ 0	$3.00	12.00%	$25.00
250,000	3.26	12.51	26.03
500,000	3.55	13.20	26.89*
750,000	3.77	14.16	26.59
1,000,000	3.90	15.60	25.00

*Maximum: Since D = $500,000 and assets = $2,000,000, optimal D/A = 25%.

What debt ratio maximizes EPS?

See preceding slide. Maximum EPS = $3.90 at D = $1,000,000, and D/A = 50%. (Remember DPS = EPS because payout = 100%.)

Risk is too high at D/A = 50%.

What is Campus Deli's optimal capital structure?

P_0 is maximized ($26.89) at D/A = $500,000/$2,000,000 = 25%, so optimal D/A = 25%.

EPS is maximized at 50%, but primary interest is stock price, not E(EPS).

The example shows that we can push up E(EPS) by using more debt, but the risk resulting from increased leverage more than offsets the benefit of higher E(EPS).

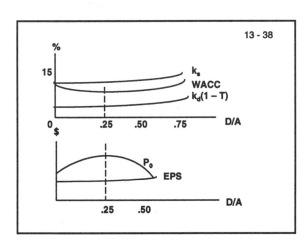

If it were discovered that the firm had more/less business risk than originally estimated, how would the analysis be affected?

If there were higher business risk, then the probability of financial distress would be greater at any debt level, and the optimal capital structure would be one that had less debt. On the other hand, lower business risk would lead to an optimal capital structure with more debt.

13 - 40

Other Factors to Consider When Establishing the Firm's Target Capital Structure

1. Industry average debt ratio
2. TIE ratios under different scenarios
3. Lender/rating agency attitudes
4. Reserve borrowing capacity
5. Effects of financing on control
6. Asset structure
7. Expected tax rate

---

13 - 41

How would these factors affect the Target Capital Structure?

1. Sales stability?
2. High operating leverage?
3. Increase in the corporate tax rate?
4. Increase in the personal tax rate?
5. Increase in bankruptcy costs?
6. Management spending lots of money on lavish perks?

---

13 - 42

---

13 - 43

■ The graph shows MM's tax benefit vs. bankruptcy cost theory.

■ Logical, but doesn't tell whole capital structure story. Main problem--assumes investors have same information as managers.

---

13 - 44

Signaling theory suggests firms should use less debt than MM suggest.

This *unused debt capacity* helps avoid stock sales, which depress P_0 because of signaling effects.

---

13 - 45

What are "signaling" effects in capital structure?

Assumptions:

■ Managers have better information about a firm's long-run value than outside investors.

■ Managers act in the best interests of current stockholders.

Therefore, managers can be expected to:

- Issue stock if they think stock is overvalued.
- Issue debt if they think stock is undervalued.

  As a result, investors view a *common stock* offering as a negative signal-- managers think stock is overvalued.

Conclusions on Capital Structure

1. Need to make calculations as we did, but should also recognize inputs are "guesstimates."
2. As a result of imprecise numbers, capital structure decisions have a large judgmental content.
3. We end up with capital structures varying widely among firms, even similar ones in same industry.

EXAM-TYPE PROBLEMS

13-1. If you know that your firm is facing relatively poor prospects but needs new capital, and you know that investors do not have this information, signaling theory would predict that you would

   a. Issue debt to maintain the returns of equity holders.

   b. Issue equity to share the burden of decreased equity returns between old and new shareholders.

   c. Be indifferent between issuing debt and equity.

   d. Postpone going into the capital markets until your firm's prospects improve.

   e. Convey your inside information to investors using the media to eliminate the information asymmetry.

13-2. Howell Enterprises is forecasting EPS of $4.00 per share for next year. The firm has 10,000 shares outstanding; it pays 12 percent interest on its debt; and it faces a 40 percent marginal tax rate. Its estimated fixed costs are $80,000, while its variable costs are estimated at 40 percent of revenues. The firm's target capital structure is 40 percent equity and 60 percent debt, and it has total assets of $400,000. On what level of sales is Howell basing its EPS forecast? ($292,445)

13-3. A company estimates that its fixed operating costs are $900,000, and its variable costs are $3.25 per unit sold. Each unit produced sells for $4.75. What is the company's breakeven point? In other words, how many units must it sell before its operating income becomes positive? (600,000)

13-4. Harris Enterprises is trying to estimate its optimal capital structure. The firm's current capital structure consists of 30 percent debt and 70 percent equity; however, management believes the firm should use more debt. The risk-free rate, k_{RF}, is 6 percent, the market risk premium, $k_M - k_{RF}$, is 5 percent, and the firm's tax rate is 40 percent. Currently, Harris' cost of equity is 12 percent, which is determined on the basis of the CAPM. What would be Harris' estimated cost of equity if it were to change from its present capital structure to a capital structure consisting of 45 percent debt and 55 percent equity? (13.12%)

14-14 Southeastern Steel Company (SSC) was formed 5 years ago to exploit a new continuous-casting process. SSC's founders, Donald Brown and Margo Valencia, had been employed in the research department of a major integrated-steel company, but when that company decided against using the new process (which Brown and Valencia had developed), they decided to strike out on their own. One advantage of the new process was that it required relatively little capital in comparison with the typical steel company, so Brown and Valencia have been able to avoid issuing new stock, and thus they own all of the shares. However, SSC has now reached the stage in which outside equity capital is necessary if the firm is to achieve its growth targets yet still maintain its target capital structure of 60 percent equity and 40 percent debt. Therefore, Brown and Valencia have decided to take the company public. Until now, Brown and Valencia have paid themselves reasonable salaries but routinely reinvested all after-tax earnings in the firm, so dividend policy has not been an issue. However, before talking with potential outside investors, they must decide on a dividend policy.

Assume that you were recently hired by Arthur Adamson & Company (AA), a national consulting firm, which has been asked to help SSC prepare for its public offering. Martha Millon, the senior AA consultant in your group, has asked you to make a presentation to Brown and Valencia in which you review the theory of dividend policy and discuss the following questions.

a. (1) What is meant by the term "dividend policy"?

   (2) The terms "irrelevance," "bird-in-the-hand," and "tax preference" have been used to describe three major theories regarding the way dividend policy affects a firm's value. Explain what these terms mean, and briefly describe each theory.

   (3) What do the three theories indicate regarding the actions management should take with respect to dividend policy?

   (4) Explain the relationships between dividend policy, stock price, and the cost of equity under each dividend policy theory by constructing two graphs such as those shown in Figure 14-1. Dividend payout should be placed on the X-axis.

   (5) What results have empirical studies of the dividend theories produced? How does all this affect what we can tell managers about dividend policy?

b. Discuss (1) the information content, or signaling, hypothesis, (2) the clientele effect, and (3) their effects on dividend policy.

c. (1) Assume that SSC has an $800,000 capital budget planned for the coming year. You have determined that its present capital structure (60 percent equity and 40 percent debt) is optimal, and its net income is forecasted at $600,000. Use the residual dividend model approach to determine SSC's total dollar dividend and payout ratio. In the process, explain what the residual dividend model is. Then, explain what would happen if net income were forecasted at $400,000, or at $800,000.

(2) In general terms, how would a change in investment opportunities affect the payout ratio under the residual payment policy?

(3) What are the advantages and disadvantages of the residual policy? (Hint: Don't neglect signaling and clientele effects.)

d. What is a dividend reinvestment plan (DRIP), and how does it work?

e. Describe the series of steps that most firms take in setting dividend policy in practice.

f. What are stock repurchases? Discuss the advantages and disadvantages of a firm's repurchasing its own shares.

g. What are stock dividends and stock splits? What are the advantages and disadvantages of stock dividends and stock splits?

CHAPTER 14
Distributions to Shareholders:
Dividends and Share Repurchases

- Theories of investor preferences
- Signaling effects
- Residual model
- Dividend reinvestment plans
- Stock dividends and stock splits
- Stock repurchases

What is "dividend policy"?

- It is the decision to pay out earnings versus retaining and reinvesting them. Dividend policy includes:

  1. High or low payout?

  2. Stable or irregular dividends?

  3. How frequent?

  4. Do we announce the policy?

Do investors prefer high or low payouts? There are three theories:

- Dividends are irrelevant: Investors don't care about payout.

- Bird in the hand: Investors prefer a high payout.

- Tax preference: Investors prefer a low payout, hence growth.

Dividend Irrelevance Theory

- Investors are indifferent between dividends and retention-generated capital gains. If they want cash, they can sell stock. If they don't want cash, they can use dividends to buy stock.
- Modigliani-Miller support irrelevance.
- Theory is based on unrealistic assumptions (no taxes or brokerage costs), hence may not be true. Need an empirical test.

Bird-in-the-Hand Theory

- Investors think dividends are less risky than potential future capital gains, hence they like dividends.
- If so, investors would value high payout firms more highly, i.e., a high payout would result in a high P_0.

Tax Preference Theory

- Retained earnings lead to long-term capital gains, which are taxed at lower rates than dividends: 20% vs. up to 39.6%. Capital gains taxes are also deferred.
- This could cause investors to prefer firms with low payouts, i.e., a high payout results in a low P_0.

14 - 7

Implications of 3 Theories for Managers

Theory	Implication
Irrelevance	Any payout OK
Bird in the hand	Set high payout
Tax preference	Set low payout

But which, if any, is correct???

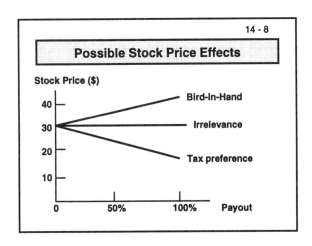

14 - 8

Possible Stock Price Effects

Stock Price ($)

- Bird-in-Hand
- Irrelevance
- Tax preference

Payout: 0, 50%, 100%

Stock Price axis: 10, 20, 30, 40

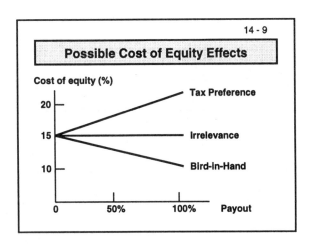

14 - 9

Possible Cost of Equity Effects

Cost of equity (%)

- Tax Preference
- Irrelevance
- Bird-in-Hand

Payout: 0, 50%, 100%

Cost of equity axis: 10, 15, 20

Which theory is most correct?

- Empirical testing has not been able to determine which theory, if any, is correct.
- Thus, managers use judgment when setting policy.
- Analysis is used, but it must be applied with judgment.

What's the "information content," or "signaling," hypothesis?

- Managers hate to cut dividends, so they won't raise dividends unless they think raise is sustainable. So, investors view dividend increases as *signals* of management's view of the future.
- Therefore, a stock price increase at time of a dividend increase could reflect higher expectations for future EPS, not a desire for dividends.

What's the "clientele effect"?

- Different groups of investors, or clienteles, prefer different dividend policies.
- Firm's past dividend policy determines its current clientele of investors.
- Clientele effects impede changing dividend policy. Taxes & brokerage costs hurt investors who have to switch companies.

What is the "residual dividend model"?

- Find the retained earnings needed for the capital budget.
- Pay out any leftover earnings (the residual) as dividends.
- This policy minimizes flotation and equity signaling costs, hence minimizes the WACC.

Using the Residual Model to Calculate Dividends Paid

$$\text{Dividends} = \frac{\text{Net}}{\text{income}} - \left[\left(\begin{array}{c} \text{Target} \\ \text{equity} \\ \text{ratio} \end{array} \right) \left(\begin{array}{c} \text{Total} \\ \text{capital} \\ \text{budget} \end{array} \right) \right].$$

Example of Residual Dividend Model

- Capital budget: $800,000. Given.
- Target capital structure: 40% debt, 60% equity. Want to maintain.
- Forecasted net income: $600,000.
- How much of the $600,000 should we pay out as dividends?

Of the $800,000 capital budget, 0.6($800,000) = $480,000 must be equity to keep at target capital structure. [0.4($800,000) = $320,000 will be debt.]

With $600,000 of net income, the residual is $600,000 − $480,000 = $120,000 = dividends paid.

Payout ratio = $120,000/$600,000
= 0.20 = 20%.

How would a drop in NI to $400,000 affect the dividend? A rise to $800,000?

- NI = $400,000: Need $480,000 of equity, so should retain the whole $400,000. Dividends = 0.

- NI = $800,000: Dividends = $800,000 − $480,000 = $320,000. Payout = $320,000/$800,000 = 40%.

How would a change in investment opportunities affect dividend under the residual policy?

- Fewer good investments would lead to smaller capital budget, hence to a higher dividend payout.

- More good investments would lead to a lower dividend payout.

Advantages and Disadvantages of the Residual Dividend Policy

- Advantages: Minimizes new stock issues and flotation costs.
- Disadvantages: Results in variable dividends, sends conflicting signals, increases risk, and doesn't appeal to any specific clientele.
- Conclusion: Consider residual policy when setting target payout, but don't follow it rigidly.

What's a "dividend reinvestment plan (DRIP)"?

- Shareholders can automatically reinvest their dividends in shares of the company's common stock. Get more stock than cash.
- There are two types of plans:
  - Open market
  - New stock

Open Market Purchase Plan

- Dollars to be reinvested are turned over to trustee, who buys shares on the open market.
- Brokerage costs are reduced by volume purchases.
- Convenient, easy way to invest, thus useful for investors.

New Stock Plan

- Firm issues new stock to DRIP enrollees, keeps money and uses it to buy assets.

- No fees are charged, plus sells stock at discount of 5% from market price, which is about equal to flotation costs of underwritten stock offering.

- Optional investments sometimes possible, up to $150,000 or so.

- Firms that need new equity capital use new stock plans.

- Firms with no need for new equity capital use open market purchase plans.

- Most NYSE listed companies have a DRIP. Useful for investors.

Setting Dividend Policy

- Forecast capital needs over a planning horizon, often 5 years.
- Set a target capital structure.
- Estimate annual equity needs.
- Set target payout based on the residual model.
- Generally, some dividend growth rate emerges. Maintain target growth rate if possible, varying capital structure somewhat if necessary.

14 - 25

Dividend Payout Ratios for Selected Industries

Industry	Payout ratio
Banking	36.62
Computer Software Services	15.61
Drug	41.49
Electric Utilities (Eastern U.S.)	64.47
Internet	n/a
Restaurants	19.29
Semiconductors	10.78
Steel	26.92
Tobacco	54.90

*None of the Internet companies included in the Value Line Investment Survey paid a dividend.

---

14 - 26

Stock Repurchases

Repurchases: Buying own stock back from stockholders.

Reasons for repurchases:

- As an alternative to distributing cash as dividends.
- To dispose of one-time cash from an asset sale.
- To make a large capital structure change.

---

14 - 27

Advantages of Repurchases

- Stockholders can tender or not.
- Helps avoid setting a high dividend that cannot be maintained.
- Repurchased stock can be used in take-overs or resold to raise cash as needed.
- Income received is capital gains rather than higher-taxed dividends.
- Stockholders may take as a positive signal--management thinks stock is undervalued.

14 - 28

Disadvantages of Repurchases

- May be viewed as a negative signal (firm has poor investment opportunities).
- IRS could impose penalties if repurchases were primarily to avoid taxes on dividends.
- Selling stockholders may not be well informed, hence be treated unfairly.
- Firm may have to bid up price to complete purchase, thus paying too much for its own stock.

14 - 29

Stock Dividends vs. Stock Splits

- Stock dividend: Firm issues new shares in lieu of paying a cash dividend. If 10%, get 10 shares for each 100 shares owned.

- Stock split: Firm increases the number of shares outstanding, say 2:1. Sends shareholders more shares.

14 - 30

Both stock dividends and stock splits increase the number of shares outstanding, so "the pie is divided into smaller pieces."

Unless the stock dividend or split conveys information, or is accompanied by another event like higher dividends, *the stock price falls so as to keep each investor's wealth unchanged.*

But splits/stock dividends may get us to an "optimal price range."

When and why should a firm consider splitting its stock?

- There's a widespread belief that the *optimal price range* for stocks is $20 to $80. Stock splits can be used to keep the price in this optimal range.
- Stock splits generally occur when management is confident, so are interpreted as *positive signals*.
- On average, stocks tend to outperform the market in the year following a split.

EXAM-TYPE PROBLEMS

14-1. If you were to argue that the firm's cost of equity, k_s, increases as the dividend payout decreases, you would be making an argument _____ with MM's dividend irrelevance theory, and _____ with Gordon and Lintner's "bird-in-the-hand" theory.

   a. consistent; consistent

   b. inconsistent; consistent

   c. consistent; inconsistent

   d. inconsistent; inconsistent

   e. The argument above does not make sense, neither theory involves the cost of equity capital.

14-2. Which of the following statements is most correct?

   a. If the *dividend irrelevance theory* (which is associated with the names Modigliani and Miller) were exactly correct, and if this theory could be tested with "clean" data, then we would find, in a regression of stock price and dividend payout, a line with a slope of -1.0.

   b. The *tax preference* and *bird-in-the-hand* theories lead to identical conclusions as to the optimal dividend policy.

   c. If a company raises its dividend by an unexpectedly large amount, the announcement of this new and higher dividend is generally accompanied by an increase in the stock price. This is consistent with the bird-in-the-hand theory, and Modigliani and Miller used these findings to support their position on dividend theory.

   d. If it could be demonstrated that a *clientele effect* exists, this would suggest that firms could alter their dividend payment policies from year to year to take advantage of investment opportunities without having to worry about the effects of changing dividends on capital costs.

   e. Each of the above statements is false.

14-3. Driver Corporation is considering a number of positive NPV projects for a total capital budget of $60 million. Its optimal capital structure is 60 percent equity and 40 percent debt. Its earnings before interest and taxes (EBIT) were $98 million for the year. The firm has $200 million in assets, pays an average of 10 percent on all its debt, and faces a marginal tax rate of 34 percent. If the firm maintains a residual dividend policy and will finance its capital budget so as to keep its optimal capital structure intact, what will be the amount of the dividends it pays out? ($23.4 million)

15-23 Dan Barnes, financial manager of Ski Equipment Inc. (SKI), is excited, but apprehensive. The company's founder recently sold his 51 percent controlling block of stock to Kent Koren, who is a big fan of EVA (Economic Value Added). EVA is found by taking the after-tax operating profit and then subtracting the dollar cost of all the capital the firm uses:

$$EVA = EBIT(1 - T) - \text{Capital costs}$$
$$= EBIT(1 - T) - WACC \text{ (Capital employed)}.$$

If EVA is positive, then the firm is creating value. On the other hand, if EVA is negative, the firm is not covering its cost of capital, and stockholders' value is being eroded. Koren rewards managers handsomely if they create value, but those whose operations produce negative EVAs are soon looking for work. Koren frequently points out that if a company can generate its current level of sales with less assets, it would need less capital. That would, other things held constant, lower capital costs and increase its EVA.

Shortly after he took control of SKI, Kent Koren met with SKI's senior executives to tell them of his plans for the company. First, he presented some EVA data that convinced everyone that SKI had not been creating value in recent years. He then stated, in no uncertain terms, that this situation must change. He noted that SKI's designs of skis, boots, and clothing are acclaimed throughout the industry, but something is seriously amiss elsewhere in the company. Costs are too high, prices are too low, or the company employs too much capital, and he wants SKI's managers to correct the problem or else.

Barnes has long felt that SKI's working capital situation should be studied—the company may have the optimal amounts of cash, securities, receivables, and inventories, but it may also have too much or too little of these items. In the past, the production manager resisted Barnes' efforts to question his holdings of raw materials inventories, the marketing manager resisted questions about finished goods, the sales staff resisted questions about credit policy (which affects accounts receivable), and the treasurer did not want to talk about her cash and securities balances. Koren's speech made it clear that such resistance would no longer be tolerated.

Barnes also knows that decisions about working capital cannot be made in a vacuum. For example, if inventories could be lowered without adversely affecting operations, then less capital would be required, the dollar cost of capital would decline, and EVA would increase. However, lower raw materials inventories might lead to production slowdowns and higher costs, while lower finished goods inventories might lead to the loss of profitable sales. So, before inventories are changed, it will be necessary to study operating as well as financial effects. The situation is the same with regard to cash and receivables.

a. Barnes plans to use the ratios in Table IC15-1 as the starting point for discussions with SKI's operating executives. He wants everyone to think about the pros and cons of changing each type of current asset and how changes would interact to affect profits and EVA. Based on the Table IC15-1 data, does SKI seem to be following a relaxed, moderate, or restricted working capital policy?

Table IC15-1. Selected Ratios: SKI and Industry Average

	SKI	Industry
Current	1.75×	2.25×
Quick	0.83×	1.20×
Debt/assets	58.76%	50.00%
Turnover of cash and securities	16.67×	22.22×
Days sales outstanding (365-day basis)	45.63	32.00
Inventory turnover	4.82×	7.00×
Fixed assets turnover	11.35×	12.00×
Total assets turnover	2.08×	3.00×
Profit margin on sales	2.07%	3.50%
Return on equity (ROE)	10.45%	21.00%

b. How can one distinguish between a relaxed but rational working capital policy and a situation in which a firm simply has a lot of current assets because it is inefficient? Does SKI's working capital policy seem appropriate?

c. Assume that SKI's payables deferral period is 30 days. Now, calculate the firm's cash conversion cycle.

d. What might SKI do to reduce its cash and securities without harming operations?

In an attempt to better understand SKI's cash position, Barnes developed a cash budget. Data for the first two months of the year are shown in Table IC15-2. (Note that Barnes' preliminary cash budget does not account for interest income or interest expense.) He has the figures for the other months, but they are not shown in Table IC15-2.

Table IC15-2. SKI's Cash Budget for January and February

		Nov	Dec	Jan	Feb	Mar	Apr
I. COLLECTIONS AND PURCHASES WORKSHEET							
(1)	Sales (gross)	$71,218	$68,212.00	$65,213.00	$52,475.00	$42,909	$30,524
Collections:							
(2)	During month of sale (0.2)(0.98)(month's sales)			12,781.75	10,285.10		
(3)	During first month after sale 0.7(previous month's sales)			47,748.40	45,649.10		
(4)	During second month after sale 0.1(sales 2 months ago)			7,121.80	6,821.20		
(5)	Total collections (Lines 2 + 3 + 4)			$67,651.95	$62,755.40		
Purchases:							
(6)	0.85(forecasted sales 2 months from now)		$44,603.75	$36,472.65	$25,945.40		
(7)	Payments (1-month lag)			44,603.75	36,472.65		
II. CASH GAIN OR LOSS FOR MONTH							
(8)	Collections (from Section I)			$67,651.95	$62,755.40		
(9)	Payments for purchases (from Section I)			44,603.75	36,472.65		
(10)	Wages and salaries			6,690.56	5,470.90		
(11)	Rent			2,500.00	2,500.00		
(12)	Taxes						
(13)	Total payments			$53,794.31	$44,443.55		
(14)	Net cash gain (loss) during month (Line 8 - Line 13)			$13,857.64	$18,311.85		
III. CASH SURPLUS OR LOAN REQUIREMENT							
(15)	Cash at beginning of month if no borrowing is done			$ 3,000.00	$16,857.64		
(16)	Cumulative cash (cash at start, + gain or - loss = Line 14 + Line 15)			16,857.64	35,169.49		
(17)	Target cash balance			1,500.00	1,500.00		
(18)	Cumulative surplus cash or loans outstanding to maintain $1,500 target cash balance (Line 16 - Line 17)			$15,357.64	$33,669.49		

e. Should depreciation expense be explicitly included in the cash budget? Why or why not?

f. In his preliminary cash budget, Barnes has assumed that all sales are collected and, thus, that SKI has no bad debts. Is this realistic? If not, how would bad debts be dealt with in a cash budgeting sense? (Hint: Bad debts will affect collections but not purchases.)

g. Barnes' cash budget for the entire year, although not given here, is based heavily on his forecast for monthly sales. Sales are expected to be extremely low between May and September but then increase dramatically in the fall and winter. November is typically the firm's best month, when SKI ships equipment to retailers for the holiday season. Interestingly, Barnes' forecasted cash budget indicates that the company's cash holdings will exceed the targeted cash balance every month except for October and November, when shipments will be high but collections will not be coming in until later. Based on the ratios in

Table IC15-1, does it appear that SKI's target cash balance is appropriate? In addition to possibly lowering the target cash balance, what actions might SKI take to better improve its cash management policies, and how might that affect its EVA?

h. What reasons might SKI have for maintaining a relatively high amount of cash?

i. What are the three categories of inventory costs? If the company takes steps to reduce its inventory, what effect would this have on the various costs of holding inventory?

j. Is there any reason to think that SKI may be holding too much inventory? If so, how would that affect EVA and ROE?

k. If the company reduces its inventory without adversely affecting sales, what effect should this have on the company's cash position (1) in the short run and (2) in the long run? Explain in terms of the cash budget and the balance sheet.

l. Barnes knows that SKI sells on the same credit terms as other firms in its industry. Use the ratios presented in Table IC15-1 to explain whether SKI's customers pay more or less promptly than those of its competitors. If there are differences, does that suggest that SKI should tighten or loosen its credit policy? What four variables make up a firm's credit policy, and in what direction should each be changed by SKI?

m. Does SKI face any risks if it tightens its credit policy?

n. If the company reduces its DSO without seriously affecting sales, what effect would this have on its cash position (1) in the short run and (2) in the long run? Answer in terms of the cash budget and the balance sheet. What effect should this have on EVA in the long run?

In addition to improving the management of its current assets, SKI is also reviewing the ways in which it finances its current assets. With this concern in mind, Dan is also trying to answer the following questions.

o. SKI tries to match the maturity of its assets and liabilities. Describe how SKI could adopt either a more aggressive or more conservative financing policy.

p. What are the advantages and disadvantages of using short-term credit as a source of financing?

q. Is it likely that SKI could make significantly greater use of accruals?

r. Assume that SKI buys on terms of 1/10, net 30, but that it can get away with paying on the 40th day if it chooses not to take discounts. Also, assume that it purchases $506,985 of equipment per year, net of discounts. How much free trade credit can the company get, how much costly trade credit can it get, and what is the percentage cost of the costly credit? Should SKI take discounts?

s. Would it be feasible for SKI to finance with commercial paper?

CHAPTER 15
Working Capital Management

- Alternative working capital policies
- Cash management
- Inventory and A/R management
- Working capital financing policies
- A/P (trade credit)
- Commercial paper

Definitions

- Gross W.C.: Total current assets.
- Net W.C.: Current assets – Current liabilities.
- W.C. Policy: Decisions as to (1) the level of each type of current asset, and (2) how current assets will be financed.
- W.C. Management: Controlling cash, inventories, and A/R, plus S-T liability management.

Selected Ratios--SKI Inc.

	SKI	Industry
Current	1.75x	2.25x
Quick	0.83x	1.20x
Debt/Assets	58.76%	50.00%
Turnover of cash & securities	16.67x	22.22x
DSO (365-day basis)	45.63	32.00
Inv. turnover	4.82x	7.00x
F. A. turnover	11.35x	12.00x
T. A. turnover	2.08x	3.00x
Profit margin	2.07%	3.50%
ROE	10.45%	21.00%

SKI appears to have large amounts of working capital given its level of sales.

How does SKI's working capital policy compare with the industry?

- Working capital policy is reflected in current ratio, quick ratio, turnover of cash and securities, inventory turnover, and DSO.

- These ratios indicate SKI has large amounts of working capital relative to its level of sales. SKI is either very conservative or inefficient.

Is SKI inefficient or just conservative?

- A conservative (relaxed) policy may be appropriate if it leads to greater profitability.

- However, SKI is not as profitable as the average firm in the industry. This suggests the company has excessive working capital.

Cash Conversion Cycle

The cash conversion model focuses on the length of time between when a company make payments to its creditors and when a company receives payment from its customers.

$$CCC = \begin{matrix} \text{Inventory} \\ \text{conversion} \\ \text{period} \end{matrix} + \begin{matrix} \text{Receivables} \\ \text{collection} \\ \text{period} \end{matrix} - \begin{matrix} \text{Payables} \\ \text{deferral} \\ \text{period} \end{matrix}.$$

Cash Conversion Cycle

$$CCC = \frac{\text{Days per year}}{\text{Inv. turnover}} + \text{Days sales outstanding} - \text{Payables deferral period}$$

$$CCC = \frac{365}{4.82} + 45.6 - 30$$

$$CCC = 75.7 + 45.6 - 30$$

$$CCC = 91.3 \text{ days.}$$

Cash doesn't earn a profit, so why hold it?

1. **Transactions:** Must have some cash to operate.
2. **Precaution:** "Safety stock." But lessened by line of credit, marketable securities.
3. **Compensating balances:** For loans and/or services provided.
4. **Speculation:** To take advantage of bargains, to take discounts, etc. Reduced by credit lines, securities.

What's the goal of cash management?

- To meet above objectives, especially to have cash for transactions, yet not have any excess cash.

- To minimize transactions balances in particular, and also needs for cash to meet other objectives.

Reducing Cash and Securities without Harming Operations

Securities could be sold off and combined with existing cash used to reduce debt, to buy back stock, or to invest in operating assets.

Cash Budget: The Primary Cash Management Tool

- Purpose: Forecasts cash inflows, outflows, and ending cash balances. Used to plan loans needed or funds available to invest.

- Timing: Daily, weekly, or monthly, depending upon purpose of forecast. Monthly for annual planning, daily for actual cash management.

Data Required for Cash Budget

1. Sales forecast.
2. Information on collections delay.
3. Forecast of purchases and payment terms.
4. Forecast of cash expenses, taxes, etc.
5. Initial cash on hand.
6. Target cash balance.

SKI's Cash Budget for January and February

	Net Cash Inflows	
	January	February
Collections	$67,651.95	$62,755.40
Purchases	44,603.75	36,472.65
Wages	6,690.56	5,470.90
Rent	2,500.00	2,500.00
Total payments	$53,794.31	$44,443.55
Net CF	$13,857.64	$18,311.85

Cash Budget (Continued)

	January	February
Cash at start if no borrowing	$ 3,000.00	$16,857.64
Net CF (slide 13)	13,857.64	18,311.85
Cumulative cash	$16,857.64	$35,169.49
Less: target cash	1,500.00	1,500.00
Surplus	$15,357.64	$33,669.49

Should depreciation be explicitly included in the cash budget?

- No. Depreciation is a noncash charge. Only cash payments and receipts appear on cash budget.
- However, depreciation does affect taxes, which appear in the cash budget.

What are some other potential cash inflows besides collections?

- Proceeds from the sale of fixed assets.
- Proceeds from stock and bond sales.
- Interest earned.
- Court settlements.

How could bad debts be worked into the cash budget?

- Collections would be reduced by the amount of the bad debt losses.
- For example, if the firm had 3% bad debt losses, collections would total only 97% of sales.
- Lower collections would lead to higher borrowing requirements.

SKI's forecasted cash budget indicates that the company's cash holdings will exceed the targeted cash balance every month, except for October and November.

- Cash budget indicates the company is holding too much cash.
- SKI could improve its EVA by either investing cash in more productive assets, or by returning cash to its shareholders.

What reasons might SKI have for maintaining a relatively high amount of cash?

- If sales turn out to be considerably less than expected, SKI could face a cash shortfall.
- A company may choose to hold large amounts of cash if it does not have much faith in its sales forecast, or if it is very conservative.
- The cash may be used, in part, to fund future investments.

Categories of Inventory Costs

- Carrying Costs: Storage and handling costs, insurance, property taxes, depreciation, and obsolescence.
- Ordering Costs: Cost of placing orders, shipping and handling costs.

(More...)

- Costs of Running Short: Loss of sales, loss of customer goodwill, and the disruption of production schedules.

Reducing the average amount of inventory generally reduces carrying costs, increases ordering costs, and may increase the costs of running short.

---

15 - 22

Is SKI holding too much inventory?

- SKI's inventory turnover (4.82) is considerably lower than the industry average (7.00). The firm is carrying a lot of inventory per dollar of sales.

- By holding excessive inventory, the firm is increasing its costs, which reduces its ROE. Moreover, this additional working capital must be financed, so EVA is also lowered.

15 - 23

If SKI reduces its inventory, without adversely affecting sales, what effect will this have on its cash position?

- Short run: Cash will increase as inventory purchases decline.

- Long run: Company is likely to take steps to reduce its cash holdings and increase its EVA.

15 - 24

Do SKI's customers pay more or less promptly than those of its competitors?

- SKI's DSO (45.6 days) is well above the industry average (32 days).

- SKI's customers are paying less promptly.

- SKI should consider tightening its credit policy in order to reduce its DSO.

Elements of Credit Policy

1. **Credit Period:** How long to pay? Shorter period reduces DSO and average A/R, but it may discourage sales.
2. **Cash Discounts:** Lowers price. Attracts new customers and reduces DSO.
3. **Credit Standards:** Tighter standards tend to reduce sales, but reduce bad debt expense. Fewer bad debts reduce DSO.
4. **Collection Policy:** How tough? Tougher policy will reduce DSO but may damage customer relationships.

Does SKI face any risk if it tightens its credit policy?

YES! A tighter credit policy may discourage sales. Some customers may choose to go elsewhere if they are pressured to pay their bills sooner.

If SKI succeeds in reducing DSO without adversely affecting sales, what effect would this have on its cash position?

- **Short run:** If customers pay sooner, this increases cash holdings.
- **Long run:** Over time, the company would hopefully invest the cash in more productive assets, or pay it out to shareholders. Both of these actions would increase EVA.

Working Capital Financing Policies

- ■ Moderate: Match the maturity of the assets with the maturity of the financing.
- ■ Aggressive: Use short-term financing to finance permanent assets.
- ■ Conservative: Use permanent capital for permanent assets and temporary assets.

Moderate Financing Policy

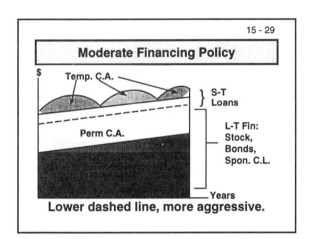

Lower dashed line, more aggressive.

Conservative Financing Policy

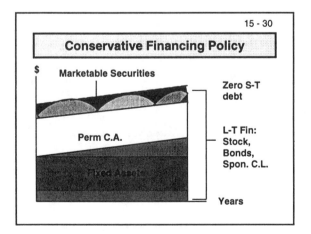

What is short-term credit, and what are the major sources?

- S-T credit: Any debt scheduled for repayment within one year.
- Major sources:
  - Accounts payable (trade credit)
  - Bank loans
  - Commercial paper
  - Accruals

- Is S-T credit riskier than L-T?

  To the company, yes. Required repayment always looms. May have trouble rolling over loans.

- Advantages of short-term credit:

  Low cost--visualize yield curve. Can get funds relatively quickly. Can repay without penalty.

Is there a cost to accruals? Do firms have much control over amount of accruals?

- Accruals are free in that no explicit interest is charged.
- Firms have little control over the level of accruals. Levels are influenced more by industry custom, economic factors, and tax laws.

15 - 34

What is trade credit?

- Trade credit is credit furnished by a firm's suppliers.
- Trade credit is often the largest source of short-term credit, especially for small firms.
- Spontaneous, easy to get, but cost can be high.

15 - 35

B&B buys $512,106 gross, or $506,985 net, on terms of 1/10, net 30, and pays on Day 40. How much free and costly trade credit, and what's the cost of costly trade credit?

Net daily purchases = $506,985/365

= $1,389.

15 - 36

Gross/Net Breakdown

- Company buys goods worth $506,985. That's the cash price.
- They must pay $5,121 more if they don't take discounts.
- Think of the extra $5,121 as a financing cost similar to the interest on a loan.
- Want to compare that cost with the cost of a bank loan.

Payables level if take discount:
Payables = $1,389(10) = **$13,890.**

Payables level if don't take discount:
Payables = $1,389(40) = **$55,560.**

Credit Breakdown:
Total trade credit   = **$55,560**
Free trade credit   = **13,890**
Costly trade credit   = **$41,670**

Nominal Cost of Costly Trade Credit

Firm loses 0.01($512,106) = $5,121 of discounts to obtain $41,670 in extra trade credit, so

$$k_{Nom} = \frac{\$5,121}{\$41,670} = 0.1229 = 12.29\%.$$

But the $5,121 is paid all *during* the year, not at year-end, so EAR rate is higher.

Nominal Cost Formula, 1/10, net 40

$$k_{Nom} = \frac{\text{Discount \%}}{1 - \text{Discount \%}} \times \frac{365 \text{ days}}{\frac{\text{Days}}{\text{taken}} - \frac{\text{Discount}}{\text{period}}}$$

$$= \frac{1}{99} \times \frac{365}{30} = 0.0101 \times 12.1667$$

$$= 0.1229 = 12.29\%.$$

Pays 1.01% 12.167 times per year.

Effective Annual Rate, 1/10, net 40

Periodic rate = 0.01/0.99 = 1.01%.

Periods/year = 365/(40 − 10) = 12.1667.

$$\text{EAR} = (1 + \text{Periodic rate})^n - 1.0$$
$$= (1.0101)^{12.1667} - 1.0 = 13.01\%.$$

Commercial Paper (CP)

- Short term notes issued by large, strong companies. B&B couldn't issue CP--it's too small.
- CP trades in the market at rates just above T-bill rate.
- CP is bought with surplus cash by banks and other companies, then held as a marketable security for liquidity purposes.

EXAM-TYPE PROBLEMS

15-1. Ziltest Company's treasurer had $1 million of excess funds that were invested in marketable securities. At the time the investment was made, it was known that the funds would be needed in 6 months to fund an ongoing construction project. Six-month T-bills with a face value of $10,000 sold for $9,708.74 to yield a 6 percent nominal annual rate. As an alternative, the treasurer could purchase 7 percent coupon, semiannual payment, 10-year Treasury bonds at par. Seeking to earn a higher yield, he purchased the T-bonds. At the end of 6 months, when the funds were needed for construction, interest rates had risen to 9.5 percent on the T-bonds. The treasurer was forced to liquidate the T-bond holdings at a lower price. What was the absolute value of the dollar difference between the T-bond's purchase price and selling price? ($154,192.20)

15-2. Which of the following statement completions is most correct? If the yield curve is upward sloping, then a firm's marketable securities portfolio, assumed to be held for liquidity purposes, should be

   a. Weighted toward long-term securities because they pay higher rates.

   b. Weighted toward short-term securities because they pay higher rates.

   c. Weighted toward U.S. Treasury securities to avoid interest rate risk.

   d. Weighted toward short-term securities to avoid interest rate risk.

   e. Balanced between long- and short-term securities to minimize the effects of either an upward or a downward shift in interest rates.

15-3. Which of the following statements is most correct?

   a. If a firm's volume of credit sales declines then its DSO will also decline.

   b. If a firm changes its credit terms from 1/20, net 40 days, to 2/10, net 60 days, the impact on sales can't be determined because the increase in the discount is offset by the longer net terms, which tends to reduce sales.

   c. The DSO of a firm with seasonal sales can vary because while the sales per day figure is usually based on the total annual sales, the accounts receivable balance will be high or low depending on the season.

   d. An aging schedule is used to determine what portion of customers pay cash and what portion buy on credit.

   e. Aging schedules can be constructed from the summary data provided in the firm's financial statements.

15-4. Jarrett Enterprises is considering whether to pursue a restricted or a relaxed current asset investment policy. The firm's annual sales are $400,000; its fixed assets are

$100,000; debt and equity are each 50 percent of total assets. EBIT is $36,000, the interest rate on the firm's debt is 10 percent, and the firm's tax rate is 40 percent. With a restricted policy, current assets will be 15 percent of sales. Under a relaxed policy, current assets will be 25 percent of sales. What is the difference in the projected ROEs between the restricted and relaxed policies? (5.4%)

15-5. Porta Stadium Inc. has annual sales of $40,000,000 and keeps average inventory of $10,000,000. On average, the firm has accounts receivable of $8,000,000. The firm buys all raw materials on credit and its trade credit terms are net 30 days. It pays on time. The firm's managers are searching for ways to shorten the cash conversion cycle. If sales can be maintained at existing levels but inventory can be lowered by $2,000,000 and accounts receivable lowered by $1,000,000, what will be the net change in the cash conversion cycle? (27.375 days shorter)

15-6. The Lasser Company needs to finance an increase in its working capital for the coming year. The firm can increase its accounts payable by not taking discounts. Lasser buys on credit terms of 1/30, net 60 days. What is the effective annual cost (not the approximate cost) of trade credit? (13.01%)

15-7 Which of the following statements is most correct?

a. Under normal conditions the shape of the yield curve implies that the interest cost of short-term debt is greater than that of long-term debt, although short-term debt has other advantages that make it desirable as a financing source.

b. Flexibility is an advantage of short-term credit but this is somewhat offset by the higher flotation costs associated with the need to repeatedly renew short-term credit.

c. A short-term loan can usually be obtained more quickly than a long-term loan but the penalty for early repayment of a short-term loan is significantly higher than for a long-term loan.

d. Statements about the flexibility, cost, and riskiness of short-term versus long-term credit are dependent on the type of credit that is actually used.

e. Short-term debt is often less costly than long-term debt and the major reason for this is that short-term debt exposes the borrowing firm to much less risk than long-term debt.

15-8. A chain of lighting fixture stores, LCG Corporation, purchases inventory with a net price of $750,000 each day. The company purchases the inventory under the credit terms of 2/20, net 50. LCG always takes the discount, but takes the full 20 days to pay its bills. What is the average accounts payable for LCG? ($15,000,000)

16-20 Citrus Products Inc. is a medium-sized producer of citrus juice drinks with groves in Indian River County, Florida. Until now, the company has confined its operations and sales to the United States, but its CEO, George Gaynor, wants to expand into the Pacific Rim. The first step would be to set up sales subsidiaries in Japan and Australia, then to set up a production plant in Japan, and, finally, to distribute the product throughout the Pacific Rim. The firm's financial manager, Ruth Schmidt, is enthusiastic about the plan, but she is worried about the implications of the foreign expansion on the firm's financial management process. She has asked you, the firm's most recently hired financial analyst, to develop a 1-hour tutorial package that explains the basics of multinational financial management. The tutorial will be presented at the next board of directors meeting. To get you started, Schmidt has supplied you with the following list of questions.

a. What is a multinational corporation? Why do firms expand into other countries?

b. What are the six major factors that distinguish multinational financial management from financial management as practiced by a purely domestic firm?

c. Consider the following illustrative exchange rates.

	U.S. Dollars Required to Buy One Unit of Foreign Currency
Japanese yen	0.009
Australian dollar	0.650

(1) Are these currency prices direct quotations or indirect quotations?

(2) Calculate the indirect quotations for yen and Australian dollars.

(3) What is a cross rate? Calculate the two cross rates between yen and Australian dollars.

(4) Assume Citrus Products can produce a liter of orange juice and ship it to Japan for $1.75. If the firm wants a 50 percent markup on the product, what should the orange juice sell for in Japan?

(5) Now, assume Citrus Products begins producing the same liter of orange juice in Japan. The product costs 250 yen to produce and ship to Australia, where it can be sold for 6 Australian dollars. What is the U.S. dollar profit on the sale?

(6) What is exchange rate risk?

d. Briefly describe the current international monetary system. How does the current system differ from the system that was in place prior to August 1971?

e. What is a convertible currency? What problems arise when a multinational company operates in a country whose currency is not convertible?

f. What is the difference between spot rates and forward rates? When is the forward rate at a premium to the spot rate? At a discount?

g. What is interest rate parity? Currently, you can exchange 1 yen for 0.0095 U.S. dollar in the 30-day forward market, and the risk-free rate on 30-day securities is 4 percent in both Japan and the United States. Does interest rate parity hold? If not, which securities offer the highest expected return?

h. What is purchasing power parity (PPP)? If grapefruit juice costs $2.00 a liter in the United States and purchasing power parity holds, what should be the price of grapefruit juice in Australia?

i. What impact does relative inflation have on interest rates and exchange rates?

j. Briefly discuss the international capital markets.

k. To what extent do average capital structures vary across different countries?

l. What is the impact of multinational operations on each of the following financial management topics?

(1) Cash management.

(2) Capital budgeting decisions.

(3) Credit management.

(4) Inventory management.

CHAPTER 16
Multinational Financial Management

- Multinational vs. domestic financial management
- Exchange rates and trading in foreign exchange
- International monetary system
- International money and capital markets

What is a multinational corporation?

A corporation that operates in two or more countries.

Why do firms expand into other countries?

1. To seek new markets.
2. To seek raw materials.
3. To seek new technology.
4. To seek production efficiency.
5. To avoid political and regulatory hurdles.
6. To diversify.

What are the six major factors that distinguish multinational from domestic financial management?

1. Different currency denominations.
2. Economic and legal ramifications.
3. Language differences.
4. Cultural differences.
5. Role of governments.
6. Political risk.

Consider the following exchange rates:

	U.S. $ to buy 1 Unit
Japanese yen	0.009
Australian dollar	0.650

■ Are these currency prices direct or indirect quotations?

● Since they are prices of foreign currencies expressed in dollars, they are direct quotations.

What is an indirect quotation?

The number of units of foreign currency needed to purchase one U.S. dollar, or the reciprocal of a direct quotation.

Calculate the indirect quotations for yen and Australian dollars.

	# of Units of Foreign Currency per U.S. $
Japanese yen	111.11
Australian dollar	1.5385

Yen: $1/0.009 = 111.11$.
A. Dollar: $1/0.650 = 1.5385$.

What is a cross rate?

The exchange rate between any two currencies. Cross rates are actually calculated on the basis of various currencies relative to the U.S. dollar.

Calculate the two cross rates between yen and Australian dollars.

■ Cross rate $= \dfrac{\text{Yen}}{\text{U.S. Dollar}} \times \dfrac{\text{U.S. Dollars}}{\text{A. Dollar}}$
$= 111.11 \times 0.650$
$= 72.22$ yen/A. dollar.

■ Cross rate $= \dfrac{\text{A. Dollars}}{\text{U.S. Dollar}} \times \dfrac{\text{U.S. Dollars}}{\text{Yen}}$
$= 1.5385 \times 0.009$
$= 0.0138$ A. dollars/yen.

Note:

- The two cross rates are reciprocals of one another.

- They can be calculated by dividing either the direct or indirect quotations.

A firm can produce a liter of orange juice and ship it to Japan for $1.75. If the firm wants a 50% markup on the product, what should the juice sell for in Japan?

Price = (1.75)(1.50)(111.11)

= 291.66 yen.

Now the firm begins producing the orange juice in Japan. The product costs 250 yen to produce and ship to Australia, where it can be sold for 6 Australian dollars. What is the U.S. dollar profit on the sale?

250 yen   = 250(0.0138) = 3.45 A. dollars.

6 – 3.45 = 2.55 Australian dollar profit.

1.5385 A. dollars = 1 U.S. dollar.

Dollar profit = 2.55/1.5385 = $1.66.

What is exchange rate risk?

The risk that the value of a cash flow in one currency translated to another currency will decline due to a change in exchange rates.

For example, in the last slide, a weakening Australian dollar (strengthening dollar) would lower the dollar profit.

Describe the current and former international monetary systems.

- The current system is a floating rate system.
- Prior to 1971, a fixed exchange rate system was in effect.
  - The U.S. dollar was tied to gold.
  - Other currencies were tied to the dollar.

The European Monetary Union

In 2002, the full implementation of the "euro" is expected to be complete. The national currencies of the 12 participating countries will be phased out in favor of the "euro." The newly formed European Central Bank will control the monetary policy of the EMU.

The 12 Member Nations of the European Monetary Union

Austria	Germany	Luxembourg
Belgium	Greece	Netherlands
Finland	Ireland	Portugal
France	Italy	Spain

European Union countries not in the EMU:
Britain   Sweden   Denmark

What is a convertible currency?

- A currency is convertible when the issuing country promises to redeem the currency at current market rates.
- Convertible currencies are traded in world currency markets.

What problems arise when a firm operates in a country whose currency is not convertible?

- It becomes very difficult for multi-national companies to conduct business because there is no easy way to take profits out of the country.
- Often, firms will barter for goods to export to their home countries.

What is the difference between spot rates and forward rates?

- Spot rates are the rates to buy currency for immediate delivery.
- Forward rates are the rates to buy currency at some agreed-upon date in the future.

When is the forward rate at a premium to the spot rate?

- If the U.S. dollar buys fewer units of a foreign currency in the forward than in the spot market, the foreign currency is selling at a premium.
- In the opposite situation, the foreign currency is selling at a discount.
- The primary determinant of the spot/forward rate relationship is relative interest rates.

What is interest rate parity?

Interest rate parity holds that investors should expect to earn the same return in all countries after adjusting for risk.

$$\frac{f_t}{e_0} = \frac{1 + k_h}{1 + k_f}.$$

f_t = t-period forward exchange rate
e_0 = today's spot rate
k_h = periodic interest rate in the home country
k_f = periodic interest rate in the foreign country

Assume 1 yen = \$0.0095 in 30-day forward market and k_{Nom} for 30-day risk-free securities in Japan and U.S. = 4%. Does interest rate parity hold?

No.

f_t = \$0.0095
k_h = 4%/12 = 0.333%
k_f = 4%/12 = 0.333%

(More...)

$$\frac{f_t}{e_0} = \frac{1+k_h}{1+k_f}$$

$$\frac{\$0.0095}{e_0} = \frac{1.0033}{1.0033}$$

$$\frac{\$0.0095}{e_0} = 1.$$

Therefore, if interest rate parity holds then e_0 = \$0.0095. However, we were given earlier that e_0 = \$0.0090.

What security offers highest return?

Japanese security.
1. Convert \$1,000 to yen in spot market. \$1,000 x 111.111 = 111,111 yen.
2. Invest 111,111 yen in 30-day Japanese security. In 30 days receive 111,111 yen x 1.00333 = 111,481 yen.
3. Agree today to exchange 111,481 yen 30 days from now at forward rate. 111,481/105.2632 = \$1,059.07.
4. 30-day return = \$59.07/\$1,000 = 5.907%, nominal annual return = 12 x 5.907% = 70.88%.

What is purchasing power parity (PPP)?

Purchasing power parity implies that the level of exchange rates adjusts so that identical goods cost the same amount in different countries.

$$P_h = P_f(e_0) \text{ or } e_0 = P_h/P_f.$$

If grapefruit juice costs $2.00/liter in U.S. and PPP holds, what is the price of grapefruit juice in Australia?

$$PPP = e_0 = P_h/P_f$$
$$\$0.6500 = \$2.00/P_f$$
$$P_f = \$2.00/\$0.6500$$
$$= 3.0769 \text{ Australian dollars.}$$

What impact does relative inflation have on interest rates and exchange rates?

- Lower inflation leads to lower interest rates, so borrowing in low-interest countries may appear attractive to multinational firms.
- However, currencies in low-inflation countries tend to appreciate against those in high-inflation rate countries, so the effective interest cost increases over the life of the loan.

Describe the international money and capital markets.

- Eurodollar markets
  - a source of dollars outside the U.S.
- International bonds
  - Foreign bonds: Sold by foreign borrower, but denominated in the currency of the country of issue.
  - Eurobonds: Sold in country other than the one in whose currency the bonds are denominated.

To what extent do average capital structures vary across different countries?

- Previous studies suggested that average capital structures vary among the large industrial countries.
- However, a recent study, which controlled for differences in accounting practices, suggests that capital structures are more similar across different countries than previously thought.

What is the impact of multinational operations on each of the following topics?

Cash Management

- Distances are greater.
- Access to more markets for loans and for temporary investments.
- Cash is often denominated in different currencies.

Capital Budgeting Decisions

- Foreign operations are taxed locally, and then funds repatriated may be subject to U.S. taxes.

- Foreign projects are subject to political risk.

- Funds repatriated must be converted to U.S. dollars, so exchange rate risk must be taken into account.

Credit Management

- Credit is more important, because commerce to lesser-developed countries often relies on credit.

- Credit for future payment may be subject to exchange rate risk.

Inventory Management

- Inventory decisions can be more complex, especially when inventory can be stored in locations in different countries.

- Some factors to consider are shipping times, carrying costs, taxes, import duties, and exchange rates.

EXAM-TYPE PROBLEMS

16-1. In 1985, a particular Japanese imported automobile sold for 1,476,000 yen or $8,200. If the car still sells for the same amount of yen today but the current exchange rate is 105 yen per dollar, what is the car selling for today in U.S. dollars? ($14,057.14)

16-2. Sunware Corporation, a U.S.-based importer, makes a purchase of crystal glassware from a firm in Germany for 39,960 marks, or $24,000, at the spot rate of 1.665 marks per dollar. The terms of the purchase are net 90 days, and the U.S. firm wants to cover this trade payable with a forward market hedge to eliminate its exchange rate risk. Suppose the firm completes a forward hedge at the 90-day forward rate of 1.682 marks. If the spot rate in 90 days is actually 1.638 marks, how much will the U.S. firm have saved in U.S. dollars by hedging its exchange rate exposure? ($638.17)

16-3. Six months ago, a Swiss investor bought a 6-month U.S. Treasury bill at a price of $9,708.74, with a maturity value of $10,000. The exchange rate at that time was 1.420 Swiss francs per dollar. Today, at maturity, the exchange rate is 1.324 for Swiss francs. What is the nominal annual rate of return to the Swiss investor? (-7.93%)

16-4. A refrigerator costs $899 in the United States. The same set costs 856 euros in France. If purchasing power parity holds, what is the spot exchange rate between the euro and the dollar? ($1.0502 per euro or 0.9522 euro per U.S. dollar)

16-5. 3-month T-bills have a nominal rate of 5 percent, while default-free Swiss bonds that mature in 3 months have a nominal rate of 3.5 percent. In the spot exchange market, one Swiss franc equals $0.6935. If interest rate parity holds, what is the 3-month forward exchange rate? ($0.6961)

SOLUTIONS TO EXAM-TYPE PROBLEMS

CHAPTER 1

1-1. d.

1-2. e.

CHAPTER 2

2-1. b.

2-2. *Florida muni bond*

A-T yield on FLA bond = 8%. (The munis are tax exempt.)

AT&T bond

A-T yield on AT&T bond = 11% − Taxes = 11% − 11%(0.4) = 6.6%.

Alternatively,

Invest $20,000 @ 11% = $2,200 interest.

Pay 40% tax, so A-T income = $2,200(1 − T) = $2,200(0.6) = $1,320.
A-T rate of return = $1,320/$20,000 = 6.6%.

AT&T preferred stock

A-T yield = 9% − Taxes = 9% − 0.3(9%)(0.4) = 9% − 1.08% = 7.92%.

Therefore, invest in the Florida muni bonds that yield 8% after taxes.

Note: This problem can be made harder by asking for the tax rate that would cause the company to prefer the AT&T bonds or the preferred stock.

2-3. a.
EBIT	$1,250,000
Interest	0
EBT	$1,250,000
Taxes (40%)	500,000
Net income	$ 750,000

b. Net cash flow = Net income + Depreciation
$$= \$750,000 + \$300,000$$
$$= \$1,050,000.$$

c. Operating cash flow = EBIT(1 − T) + Depreciation
$$= \$1,250,000(0.6) + \$300,000$$
$$= \$1,050,000.$$

d. NOPAT = EBIT(1 − T)
$$= \$1,250,000(1 − 0.4)$$
$$= \$750,000.$$

e. FCF = NOPAT − Net investment in operating capital
$$= \$750,000 − \$500,000$$
$$= \$250,000.$$

CHAPTER 3

3-1. ROE = Profit margin × Total assets turnover × Equity multiplier
        = NI/Sales × Sales/TA × TA/Equity.

Now we need to determine the inputs for the equation from the data that were given. On the left we set up an income statement, and we put numbers in it on the right:

Sales (given)	$20,000
Cost	NA
EBIT (given)	$ 2,000
Interest (given)	500
EBT	$ 1,500
Taxes (30%)	450
Net income	$ 1,050

Now we can use some ratios to get some more data:

Total assets turnover = S/TA = 2.5 (given).

D/A = 70%, so E/A = 30%, and therefore A/E = 1/(E/A) = 1/0.3 = 3.33.

Now we can complete the Du Pont equation to determine ROE:
ROE = $1,050/$20,000 × 2.5 × 3.33 = 43.75%.

3-2. a. Current NI = 0.05 × $5,000,000 = $250,000.

Current ROE = NI/Equity = $250,000/$4,000,000 = 6.25%.

Current DSO = Receivables/(Sales/365)
= $2,250,000/($5,000,000/365) = 164.25 days.

Reduce DSO to 60 days.

Freed up cash = 104.25 × $5,000,000/365 = $1,428,082.

Alternatively,

Accounts receivable/($5,000,000/365) = 60
Accounts receivable = $821,918.

Δ in A/R = $2,250,000 − $821,918 = $1,428,082.

Reduce Common Equity: $4,000,000 − $1,428,082 = $2,571,918.

New ROE = $250,000/$2,571,918 = 9.72%.

Change in ROE = 9.72% − 6.25% = +3.47%.

b. (1) Doubling the dollar amounts would not affect the answer; it would still be +3.47%.

(2) Target DSO = 70 days.
Freed up cash = 94.25 × $5,000,000/365 = $1,291,096.

Reduce Common Equity: $4,000,000 − $1,291,096 = $2,708,904.

New ROE = $250,000/$2,708,904 = 9.23%.

Change in ROE = 9.23% − 6.25% = +2.98%.

(3) Sales/Receivables = 6
$5,000,000/Receivables = 6
Receivables = $5,000,000/6 = $833,333.

Δ in AR = $2,250,000 − $833,333 = $1,416,667.

Reduce Common Equity: $4,000,000 − $1,416,667 = $2,583,333.

New ROE = $250,000/$2,583,333 = 9.68%.

Change in ROE = 9.68% − 6.25% = +3.43%.

(4) Original EPS = NI/Shares = $250,000/250,000 = $1.00.

New EPS calculation: Assume Book value = Market value. (M/B = 1.)

Price = $4,000,000/250,000 shares = $16. Stock is selling for $16 per share.

Thus, must buy back $\dfrac{\$1,428,082}{\$16}$ = 89,255 shares.

Number of shares outstanding = 250,000 − 89,255
= 160,745 shares.

New EPS = $\dfrac{\$250,000}{160,745}$ = $1.56.

Δ in EPS = $1.56 − $1.00 = +$0.56 per share.

(5) From Part 4, Book value = $16 per share. Market value = 2 × $16 = $32.

Thus, firm must buy back $1,428,082/$32 = 44,628 shares.

Number of shares outstanding = 250,000 − 44,628 = 205,372 shares.

New EPS = $250,000/205,372 = $1.22.

Δ in EPS = $1.22 − $1.00 = +$0.22 per share.

c. We could have started with lower receivables and higher fixed assets or inventory, then had you calculate the fixed assets or inventory turnover ratios. Then, we could have the company move to lower fixed assets or inventory turnover reducing equity by like amounts, and then had you determine the effects on ROE and EPS under different conditions. In any of these cases, we could have used the funds generated to retire debt, which would have lowered interest charges, and consequently, increased net income and EPS. (Note that information would have had to be given on interest and EBIT too.)

If we had to increase assets, then we would have had to finance this increase by adding either debt or equity, which would have lowered ROE and EPS, other things held constant.

3-3. a.

3-4. TIE = EBIT/I, so find EBIT and I.
Interest = \$800,000 × 0.1 = \$80,000.
Net income = \$3,200,000 × 0.06 = \$192,000.
Pre-tax income = \$192,000/(1 − T) = \$192,000/0.6 = \$320,000.
EBIT = \$320,000 + \$80,000 = \$400,000.
TIE = \$400,000/\$80,000 = 5.0×.

3-5. Before:
Equity multiplier = 1/(1 − D/A) = 1/(1 − 0.5) = 2.0.
ROE = (PM)(Assets turnover)(EM) = (10%)(0.25)(2.0) = 5%.

After:
ROE = 2(5%) = 10%
10% = (12%)(0.25)(EM)
EM = 3.33.

$$\frac{A}{E} = \frac{3.33}{1.00}$$
$$A = D + E$$
$$3.33 = D + 1.00$$
$$D = 2.33.$$

D/A = 2.33/3.33 = 0.70 = 70%.

3-6. a. $ROA = \dfrac{NI}{S} \times \dfrac{S}{A}$

$12.5\% = 3\% \times \dfrac{S}{A}$

$\dfrac{S}{A} = 4.167.$

b. $ROE = \dfrac{NI}{S} \times \dfrac{S}{A} \times \dfrac{A}{E}$

$16\% = 3\% \times 4.167 \times EM$
$EM = 1.28.$

c. From Part b, we know that A/E = 1.28; therefore, the firm's ratio of equity to assets is 1/1.28 = 0.78125 ≈ 78%. Consequently, the firm's debt ratio = D/A = 1 − E/A = 1 − 0.78 = 0.22 = 22%.

CHAPTER 4

4-1. **Formula solution:**

Step 1: *Use the AFN formula to calculate AFN.*

$$AFN = A^*/S_0(\Delta S) - L^*/S_0(\Delta S) - M(S_1)(RR)$$
$$= \frac{\$10,000}{\$10,000}(\$5,000) - \frac{\$1,500}{\$10,000}(\$5,000) - 0.11(\$15,000)(0.4)$$
$$= 1(\$5,000) - 0.15(\$5,000) - 0.11(\$15,000)(0.4)$$
$$= \$5,000 - \$750 - \$660 = \$3,590.$$

Step 2: *Calculate the new account levels for current assets and current liabilities.*

Current assets will increase by ($7,000/$10,000)($15,000) = $10,500.

The AFN will be funded using short-term debt.

Current liabilities will increase to:

A/P + Accruals = ($1,500/$10,000)($15,000)	= $2,250
S-T Debt = $2,000 + $3,590	= 5,590
Total C.L.	= $7,840

Step 3: *Calculate the new current ratio.*

New current ratio = $10,500/$7,840 = 1.34.

4-2. Construct a partial projected income statement and balance sheet:

	Last Year	Forecast Basis[a]	First Pass	AFN	Second Pass
EBIT	$ 240,000	×1.10	$ 264,000		
Interest	80,000		80,000		
EBT	$ 160,000		$ 184,000		
Taxes (40%)	64,000		73,600		
NI	$ 96,000		$ 110,400		$ 110,400
NI avail. to common	$ 96,000		$ 110,400		
Divs. to common					
(37,800 × $1.27)	48,006	37,800 × $1.40	52,920		
Addition to RE	$ 47,994		$ 57,480		$ 57,480
Total assets	$1,100,000	×1.10	$1,210,000		$1,210,000

	Last Year	Forecast Basis[a]	First Pass	AFN	Second Pass
Accruals	$ 13,636	0.0182	$ 15,000		$ 15,000
Long-term debt	640,000		640,000	+30,694	670,694
Equity	335,000		335,000	+20,462	355,462
RE	111,364	+57,480	168,844		168,844
Total liab & equity	$1,100,000		$1,158,844		$1,210,000
AFN[b]			$ 51,156		

Notes:

[a]Operating income is increased by 10%. Assets and accruals are divided by last year's sales to determine the appropriate ratio to apply to next year's sales to calculate next year's account balances.

[b]AFN financing:

The shortfall will be financed in accordance with the target capital structure.

Long-term debt	$0.60 \times \$51,156 =$	$\$30,694$
Common stock	$0.40 \times \$51,156 =$	$\underline{20,462}$
		$\$51,156$

4-3. d.

CHAPTER 5

5-1. b.

5-2. First, note that we will use the equation $k_t = 4\% + IP_t + MRP_t$. We have the data needed to find the IPs:

$IP_5 = (9\% + 6\% + 4\% + 4\% + 4\%)/5 = 27\%/5 = 5.4\%.$

$IP_2 = (9\% + 6\%)/2 = 7.5\%.$

Now we can substitute into the equation:

$k_5 = 4\% + 5.4\% + MRP = 12\%.$

$k_2 = 4\% + 7.5\% + MRP = 12\%.$

Now we can solve for the MRPs, and find the difference between them:

$MRP_5 = 12\% - 9.4\% = 2.6\%.$

$MRP_2 = 12\% - 11.5\% = 0.5\%.$

Difference $= 2.6\% - 0.5\% = +2.1\%.$

5-3. $k_{T-8} = 6.6\%$; $k_{C-8} = 9.3\%$; $LP_{C-8} = 0.6\%$.

$k = k^* + IP + DRP + LP + MRP$.

$k_{T-8} = 6.6\% = k^* + IP + MRP$; $DRP = LP = 0$.

$k_{C-8} = 9.3\% = k^* + IP + MRP + 0.6\% + DRP$.

Because both bonds are 8-year bonds the inflation premium and maturity risk premium on both bonds are equal. The only difference between them is the liquidity and default risk premiums.

$k_{C-8} = 9.3\% = k^* + IP + MRP + 0.6\% + DRP$.

But we know from above that $k^* + IP + MRP = 6.6\%$; therefore,

$k_{C-8} = 9.3\% = 6.6\% + 0.6\% + DRP$
$\qquad DRP = 2.1\%$.

CHAPTER 6

6-1. a.

6-2. c.

6-3. Before: $1.15 = 0.95(b_R) + 0.05(1.0)$
$\qquad\qquad 0.95(b_R) = 1.10$
$\qquad\qquad\qquad b_R = 1.15789$.

After: $b_p = 0.95(b_R) + 0.05(2.0) = 1.10 + 0.10 = 1.20$.

6-4. Electro b = 1.7; Flowers Galore b = 0.6; $k_M = 14\%$; $k_{RF} = 7.8\%$.

Electro k $= k_{RF} + (k_M - k_{RF})b$
$\qquad\quad = 7.8\% + (14\% - 7.8\%)1.7$
$\qquad\quad = 18.34\%$.

Flowers Galore k $= k_{RF} + (k_M - k_{RF})b$
$\qquad\qquad\qquad = 7.8\% + (14\% - 7.8\%)0.6$
$\qquad\qquad\qquad = 11.52\%$.

$\Delta k = 18.34\% - 11.52\%$
$\quad\;\; = +6.82\%$.

CHAPTER 7

7-1.   d.

7-2.   **Time line:**

Tabular solution:

Price of car on 27th birthday.

$$FV = \$25,000(FVIF_{10\%, 7}) = \$25,000(1.9487) = \$48,718.$$

Annual investment required.

$$FV \text{ of annuity} = FVA_n = PMT(FVIFA_{I, n})$$
$$\$48,718 = PMT(FVIFA_{14\%, 7})$$
$$PMT = \$48,718/10.7305 = \$4,540.14.$$

Financial calculator solution:

Price of car on 27th birthday.

Inputs: N = 7; I = 10; PV = -25000; PMT = 0.
Output: FV = $48,717.93 ≈ $48,718.

Annual investment required.

Inputs: N = 7; I = 14; PV = 0; FV = 48718.
Output: PMT = -$4,540.15.

7-3. Time line:

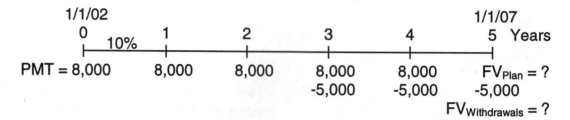

Tabular solution:

Easy way. $5,000(FVIFA_{10\%, 3}) = \$5,000(3.3100) = \$16,550.$

Hard way. Target FV = $8,000(FVIFA_{10\%, 5})(1.10) = \$53,725.$ Find FV of cash flow stream of $8,000 for Years 0-2; $3,000 for Years 3-4; and -$5,000 for Year 5; and subtract from $53,725. The answer is $16,550.

Financial calculator solution:

Calculate the FV of the withdrawals, which is how much her actual account fell short of her plan.

END mode   Inputs: N = 3; I = 10; PV = 0; PMT = -5000.
                      Output: FV = $16,550.

Alternative solution:

Calculate FV of original plan.

BEGIN mode   Inputs: N = 5; I = 10; PV = 0; PMT = -8000.
                      Output: FV = $53,724.88.

Calculate FV of actual deposit less withdrawals, take the difference.

Inputs: CF_0 = 8000; CF_1 = 8000; N_j = 2; CF_2 = 3000; N_j = 2; CF_3 = -5000; I = 10.
Outputs: NFV = $37,174.88.

Difference: $53,724.88 – $37,174.88 = $16,550.

7-4. **Time line:**

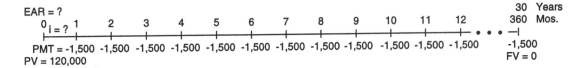

EAR = ?
0 I = ? 1   2   3   4   5   6   7   8   9   10   11   12   30 Years / 360 Mos.

PMT = -1,500 -1,500 -1,500 -1,500 -1,500 -1,500 -1,500 -1,500 -1,500 -1,500 -1,500 -1,500   -1,500
PV = 120,000   FV = 0

Financial calculator solution:

Calculate periodic rate.

Inputs: N = 360; PV = 120000; PMT = -1500; FV = 0.
Output: I = 1.235% per period.

Use interest rate conversion feature.

Inputs: NOM% = 1.235 × 12 = 14.82; P/YR = 12.
Output: EFF% = 15.868% ≈ 15.87%.

7-5. **Steps:**

1. He will save for 10 years, then receive payments for 25 years.

2. He wants a payment of $40,000 per year in today's dollars for the first payment only. Real income will decline. Inflation will be 5%. Enter N = 10, I = 5, PV = -40000, PMT = 0, and press FV to get FV = $65,155.79.

3. He now has $100,000 in an account that pays 8%, annual compounding. We need to find the FV of the $100,000 after 10 years. Enter N = 10, I = 8, PV = -100000, PMT = 0, and press FV to get FV = $215,892.50.

4. He wants to withdraw, or have payments of, $65,155.79 per year for 25 years, with the first payment made at the beginning of the first retirement year. So, we have a 25-year annuity due with PMT = $65,155.79, at an interest rate of 8%. (The interest rate is 8% annually, so no adjustment is required.) Set the calculator to BEGIN MODE, then enter N = 25, I = 8, PMT = 65155.79, FV = 0, and press PV to get PV = $751,165.35. This amount must be on hand to make the 25 payments.

5. Since the original $100,000, which grows to $215,892.50, will be available, we must save enough to accumulate $751,165.35 − $215,892.50 = $535,272.85.

6. The $535,272.85 is the FV of a 10-year ordinary annuity. The payments will be deposited in the bank and earn 8% interest. Therefore, set the calculator to END MODE and enter N = 10, I = 8, PV = 0, FV = 535272.85, and press PMT to find PMT = $36,949.61 ≈ $36,950.

7-6.   a. $i_{PER} = \dfrac{i_{Nom}}{m}$

   $= \dfrac{0.10}{4} = 0.025 = 2.5\%.$

   b. i_{Nom} = stated interest = 10%.

   c. $EAR = \left(1 + \dfrac{i_{Nom}}{m}\right)^m - 1$

   $= \left(1 + \dfrac{0.10}{4}\right)^4 - 1$

   $= 0.1038 = 10.38\%.$

CHAPTER 8

8-1.   Time line:

Investors would expect to earn either the YTM or the YTC, and the expected return on the old bonds is the cost GSU would have to pay in order to sell new bonds.

Financial calculator solution:

Calculate the YTM on the old bonds.

Inputs: N = 2(30) = 60; PV = -676.77; PMT = 80/2 = 40; FV = 1000.
Output: I = 6% = $k_d/2$. 6% is the semiannual or periodic rate.

YTM = 2(6%) = 12%.

Calculate the YTC for comparison.

Inputs: N = 2(5) = 10; PV = -676.77; PMT = 80/2 = 40; FV = 1080.
Output: I = 9.70% = k$_d$/2.

YTC = 2(9.70%) = 19.40%.

Would investors expect the company to call the bonds? No. The company currently pays interest of only 8% on its debt. New debt would cost GSU at least 12%. It would be foolish for the company to call the bonds, because investors would logically expect to earn the current YTM of 12% on new bonds. So k$_d$ = 12% is the best estimate of the nominal annual interest rate GSU would have to pay on the new bonds.

8-2. **Time line:**

Financial calculator solution:

We are comparing securities with different payment patterns, semiannual and quarterly. To properly value the student loan securities, we must match the opportunity cost rate on the bonds with the payment period on the student loan securities, which is semiannual. Thus, convert the quarterly (periodic) rate on the bonds to a semiannual effective rate.

    Since the bonds are selling at par value, the 9% coupon rate is also the market rate. The semiannual periodic rate is then 9%/2 = 4.5%. There are 2 compounding periods (quarters) in a half year.

Calculate the opportunity cost semiannual EAR of the quarterly payment bonds (using the interest rate conversion feature).

Inputs: P/YR = 2; NOM% = 9/2 = 4.5.
Output: EFF% = 4.55% = semiannual effective rate.

Calculate the present value of the student loan package, V$_B$, using the semiannual effective rate (using cash flow register).

Inputs: CF$_0$ = 0; CF$_1$ = 40; N$_j$ = 10; CF$_2$ = 50; N$_j$ = 13; CF$_3$ = 1050; I = 4.55.
Output: NPV = V$_B$ = $985.97.

8-3. **Time line:**

Calculate the nominal yield to call.

The bonds are selling at a premium because the coupon interest rate is above the market rate. Under the expectation of a flat yield curve, the bonds will most likely be called so that the firm can issue new, cheaper bonds. The FV is the call price and the period is 5 years or 10 semiannual periods.

Financial calculator solution:

Calculate the semiannual interest rate and convert to a nominal annual rate.

Inputs: N = 10; PV = -1230.51; PMT = 60; FV = 1080.
Output: I = 3.85% periodic rate (semiannual).

The nominal annual rate equals 2 × 3.85% = 7.70%. Thus, the before-tax cost of debt is 7.70%.

8-4. **Time line:**

Financial calculator solution:

Calculate the original YTM when the bonds were issued.

Inputs: N = 20; PV = -214.50; PMT = 0; FV = 1000.
Output: I = 8.0%.

Calculate the current market rate using the current market price of $239.39.

Inputs: N = 15; PV = -239.39; PMT = 0; FV = 1000.
Output: I = 10.0%.

At a current market price of $239.39, market rates are 10%. Since market rates have risen, the bond will not likely be called. So today, at Year 5, the YTM of 10% is the most likely annual rate of return an investor who purchases the bonds today will earn.

8-5. e.

8-6. d.

8-7. **Time line:**

Financial calculator solution:

Calculate the PV of the bond so the current yield can then be calculated.

Inputs: N = 2 × 10 = 20; I = 12/2 = 6; PMT = 100/2 = 50; FV = 1000.
Output: PV = $885.30.

Calculate the current yield.

$$\text{Current yield} = \frac{\text{Interest}}{\text{Bond value}} = \frac{\$100}{\$885.30} = 11.30\%.$$

CHAPTER 9

9-1.   Step 1: *Calculate required rate of return.*

$$k_s = \frac{\$2}{\$20} + 6\% = 10\% + 6\% = 16\%.$$

Step 2: *Calculate risk-free rate.*

$$16\% = k_{RF} + (15\% - k_{RF})1.2$$
$$k_{RF} = 10\%.$$

Step 3: *Calculate capital gain.*

New $k_s = 10\% + (15\% - 10\%)0.6 = 13\%$.

$$\hat{P}_{New} = \frac{\$2}{0.13 - 0.06} = \$28.57.$$

Therefore, the percentage capital gain is approximately 43%, as calculated below:

$$\text{Capital gain} = \frac{\$28.57 - \$20.00}{\$20.00} = \frac{\$8.57}{\$20.00} = 0.4285 \approx 43\%.$$

9-2. **Time line:**

$\hat{P}_0 = \underline{\$71.538} \approx \$71.54.$

Tabular solution:

$\hat{P}_0 = \$0.48(\text{PVIF}_{10\%, 1}) + \$0.576(\text{PVIF}_{10\%, 2}) + \$0.6912(\text{PVIF}_{10\%, 3}) + \$93.3125(\text{PVIF}_{10\%, 3})$
   $= \$0.48(0.9091) + \$0.576(0.8264) + \$0.6912(0.7513) + \$93.3125(0.7513)$
   $= \$0.436 + \$0.476 + \$0.519 + \$70.106 = \$71.54.$

Financial calculator solution:

Inputs: $CF_0 = 0$; $CF_1 = 0.48$; $CF_2 = 0.576$; $CF_3 = 94.001$; $I = 10$.
Output: NPV = $\hat{P}_0 = \$71.54.$

9-3. e.

9-4. $\hat{k}_p = \dfrac{D_p}{V_p}$

$0.125 = \dfrac{\$8.75}{V_p}$

$V_p = \$70.$

9-5. $FCF_1 = EBIT(1 - T) + Depreciation - \begin{matrix} Capital \\ expenditures \end{matrix} - \Delta \begin{pmatrix} Net\ operating \\ working\ capital \end{pmatrix}$

$= \$800,000,000 + \$160,000,000 - \$320,000,000 - \$0$

$= \$640,000,000.$

$Firm\ value = \dfrac{FCF_1}{WACC - g}$

$= \dfrac{\$640,000,000}{0.09 - 0.04}$

$= \dfrac{\$640,000,000}{0.05}$

$= \$12,800,000,000.$

This is the total firm value. Now find the market value of its equity.

$MV_{Total} = MV_{Equity} + MV_{Debt}$

$\$12,800,000,000 = MV_{Equity} + \$4,800,000,000$

$MV_{Equity} = \$8,000,000,000.$

This is the market value of all the equity. Divide by the number of shares to find the price per share. $\$8,000,000,000/320,000,000 = \$25.00.$

CHAPTER 10

10-1. Time line:

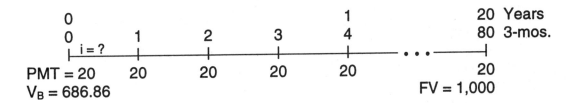

Financial calculator solution:

Calculate the __nominal__ YTM of the bond.

Inputs: $N = 4 \times 20 = 80$; $PV = -686.86$; $PMT = 80/4 = 20$; $FV = 1000$.
Output: $I = 3.05\%$ periodic rate = quarterly rate.

Nominal annual rate = $3.05\% \times 4 = 12.20\%$.

Calculate k_d after-tax. $k_{d, AT} = 12.20\%(1 - T) = 12.20\%(1 - 0.4) = 7.32\%$.

10-2. Information given:

Debt = 0.4; Equity = 0.6; $P_0 = \$28$; $D_0 = \$2.20$; $g = 6\%$; $F = 15\%$.

Use the dividend growth model to calculate k_e.

$$k_e = \frac{D_0(1+g)}{P_0(1-F)} + g = \frac{\$2.20(1.06)}{\$28(1-0.15)} + 0.06 = \frac{\$2.33}{\$23.80} + 0.06$$
$$= 0.0980 + 0.06 = 0.1580 = 15.8\%.$$

10-3. Step 1:   *Calculate the cost of common stock, k_s.*

$$k_s = \frac{D_1}{P_0} + g = \frac{\$3.00(1.10)}{\$42.50} + 0.10$$
$$= \frac{\$3.30}{\$42.50} + 0.10 = 0.0776 + 0.10 = 0.1776 = 17.76\%.$$

Step 2:   *Use the target capital structure weights to calculate WACC.*

$$WACC = 0.55(0.10)(1 - 0.35) + 0.45(17.76\%) = 11.57\%.$$

10-4. Debt = 42%; Equity = 58%; YTM = 11%; T = 40%; WACC = 10.53%.
$k_s = ?$

$k_d (1 - T) = 11\%(1 - 0.4) = 6.6\%$.

$WACC = w_d k_d(1 - T) + w_c k_s$
$10.53\% = 0.42(6.6\%) + (0.58)k_s$
$7.758\% = (0.58)k_s$
  $k_s = 13.38\%$.

CHAPTER 11

11-1. Time line:

Cash flows: S   -1,100   900   350   50   10

$NPV_S = ?$ $IRR_S = ?$

Cash flows: L   -1,100   0   300   500   850

$NPV_L = ?$ $IRR_L = ?$

Financial calculator solution:

Calculate the NPV and IRR of each project, and then select the IRR of the higher NPV project.

Project S: Inputs: $CF_0 = -1100$; $CF_1 = 900$; $CF_2 = 350$; $CF_3 = 50$; $CF_4 = 10$; $I = 12$.
Output: $NPV_S = \$24.53$; $IRR_S = 13.88\%$.

Project L: Inputs: $CF_0 = -1100$; $CF_1 = 0$; $CF_2 = 300$; $CF_3 = 500$; $CF_4 = 850$; $I = 12$.
Output: $NPV_L = \$35.24$; $IRR_L = 13.09\%$.

Project L has the higher NPV and its IRR = 13.09%.

11-2. Time line:

	0	1	2	3	4 Years
CF_X	-100	50	40	30	10
CF_Z	-100	10	30	40	60
CF_{X-Z}	0	40	10	-10	-50

Financial calculator solution:

Calculate the IRR of each project.

Project X:

Inputs: $CF_0 = -100$; $CF_1 = 50$; $CF_2 = 40$; $CF_3 = 30$; $CF_4 = 10$.
Output: IRR = 14.489% ≈ 14.49%.

Project Z:

Inputs: $CF_0 = -100$; $CF_1 = 10$; $CF_2 = 30$; $CF_3 = 40$; $CF_4 = 60$.
Output: IRR = 11.79%.

Calculate the NPVs of the projects at k = 0 discount rate.

$NPV_{X, k = 0\%} = -\$100 + \$50 + \$40 + \$30 + \$10 = \$30$.

$NPV_{Z, k = 0\%} = -\$100 + \$10 + \$30 + \$40 + \$60 = \$40$.

Calculate the IRR of the residual project cash flows, i.e., Project$_{X - Z}$.

IRR_{X-Z}: Inputs: $CF_0 = 0$; $CF_1 = 40$; $CF_2 = 10$; $CF_3 = -10$; $CF_4 = -50$.
            Output: IRR = 7.167% ≈ 7.17%.

Using the calculator we can determine that the two NPV profiles cross in the relevant part of the NPV profile graph. Project X has the higher IRR. Project Z has the higher NPV at k = 0. The crossover rate is 7.17%.

11-3. Time line:

PV of costs   -2,028   1,000   1,000   1,000
                                                    1,160.00
                                                    1,345.60
                              Terminal value (TV) =3,505.60

PV of TV = 2,028
NPV = 0 ◄──────────────── MIRR = ?

Step 1: *Calculate the historical beta.*

Regression method; Financial calculator: Different calculators have different list entry procedures and key stroke sequences.

Enter Nulook returns as the y-list:
Inputs: Item(1) = 9 INPUT; Item(2) = 15 INPUT; Item(3) = 36 INPUT.

Enter market returns as the x-list:
Inputs: Item(1) = 6 INPUT; Item(2) = 10 INPUT; Item(3) = 24 INPUT; use linear model.
Output: **m** or slope = 1.50 = historical beta.

Graphical/numerical method: Note that this method works precisely in this problem because the data points lie in a straight line. If the plotted data points don't lie in a straight line, regression is a better method.

Slope = Rise/Run = (36 − 9)/(24 − 6) = 27/18 = 1.5. Beta = 1.5.

Step 2: *Calculate the cost of equity using CAPM and beta, given inputs.*

$k_s = k_{RF} + (RP_M)b = 7.0\% + (6.0\%)1.5 = 16.0\%.$

Step 3: *Calculate MIRR.*

Financial calculator solution:

Terminal value using TVM:
Inputs: N = 3; I = 16; PV = 0; PMT = -1000.
Output: FV = $3,505.60.

Terminal value using cash flows:
Inputs: CF_0 = 0; CF_1 = 1000; N_j = 3; I = 16.
Output: NFV = $3,505.60.

Note: Some calculators do not have the Net Future Value (NFV) function. You can still calculate the NFV or terminal value using cash flows to calculate NPV, then TVM to calculate NFV or TV from the NPV.

Calculate *NPV of cash inflows.*

Inputs: $CF_0 = 0$; $CF_1 = 1000$; $N_j = 3$; $I = 16$.
Output: NPV = -$2,245.89.

Now take the NPV of $2,245.89 and bring it forward at 16% for three periods to get the FV or terminal value.

Inputs: $N = 3$; $I = 16$; PV = -2245.89; PMT = 0.
Output: FV = $3,505.60.

MIRR using TVM:
Inputs: $N = 3$; PV = -2028; PMT = 0; FV = 3505.60.
Output: $I = 20.01\% = $ MIRR $\approx 20\%$.

CHAPTER 12

12-1. E(NPV) = 0.20(-$9,000) + 0.45($20,500) + 0.35($45,675)
     = -$1,800 + $9,225 + $15,986.25
     = $23,411.25.

Since the NPV numbers are in thousands of dollars, E(NPV) = $23,411,250.

σ_{NPV} = [0.20(-$9,000 - $23,411.25)^2 + 0.45($20,500 - $23,411.25)^2
     + 0.35($45,675 - $23,411.25)^2]$^{1/2}$
     = [$210,097,825.31 + $3,813,919.45 + $173,486,097.42]$^{1/2}$
     = $19,682.42.

Since the NPV numbers are in thousands of dollars, σ_{NPV} = $19,682,424.70.

$CV_{NPV} = \dfrac{\$19,682,424.70}{\$23,411,250} = 0.8407.$

12-2. The net cost is $630,000:

Price	($540,000)
Modification	(62,500)
Increase in NOWC	(27,500)
Cash outlay for new machine	($630,000)

The operating cash flows follow:

	Year 1	Year 2	Year 3
After-tax savings[1]	$143,000	$143,000	$143,000
Depreciation tax savings[2]	69,589	94,894	31,631
Net cash flow	$212,589	$237,894	$174,631

Notes:

[1]The after-tax cost savings is $220,000(1 − T) = $220,000(0.65)
= $143,000.

[2]The depreciation expense in each year is the depreciable basis, $602,500, times the MACRS allowance percentages of 0.33, 0.45, and 0.15 for Years 1, 2, and 3, respectively. Depreciation expense in Years 1, 2, and 3 is $198,825, $271,125, and $90,375. The depreciation tax savings is calculated as the tax rate (35 percent) times the depreciation expense in each year.

The terminal cash flow is $50,702:

Salvage value	$325,000
Tax on SV*	(98,989)
Return of NOWC	27,500
	$253,511

BV in Year 4 = $602,500(0.07) = $42,175.

*Tax on SV = ($325,000 − $42,175)(0.35) = $98,989.

The project has an NPV of $54,202; thus, it should be accepted.

```
 0          1          2          3
    12%
├─────────┼──────────┼──────────┤
-630,000  212,589   237,894    174,631
                               253,511
                               428,142
```

With a financial calculator, input the appropriate cash flows into the cash flow register, input I = 12, and then solve for NPV = $54,202.

12-3. a.

0 $\xrightarrow{10\%}$ 1   2   3   4   Years

-13.6   6.8   6.8   6.8   6.8

NPV = $7.9551 million.

b. Wait 2 years:

	0	1	2	3	4	5	6	NPV @ Yr. 0
10% Prob.	0	0	-15.3	3.74	3.74	3.74	3.74	-$2.8469
90% Prob.	0	0	-15.3	7.14	7.14	7.14	7.14	6.0602

If the cash flows are only $3.74 million, the NPV of the project is negative and, thus, would not be undertaken. The value of the option of waiting two years is evaluated as 0.10($0) + 0.90($6.0602) = $5.4542 million.

Since the NPV of waiting two years is less than going ahead and proceeding with the project today, it makes sense to drill today.

CHAPTER 13

13-1. b.

13-2. $EPS_1 = \left[\left(Sales - \dfrac{Variable}{costs} - \dfrac{Fixed}{costs} - Interest\right)(1-T)\right]/Shares\ outstanding.$

Step 1: *Calculate the amount of debt and interest expense.*

Debt = 0.60 × $400,000 = $240,000.

Interest = 0.12 × $240,000 = $28,800.

Step 2: *Solve for sales using the forecasted EPS.*

EPS_1 = $4.00 = [(S − 0.40S − $80,000 − $28,800)(1 − 0.40)]/10,000
$4.00 = [(0.60S − $108,800)(0.6)]/10,000
$4.00 = (0.36S − $65,280)/10,000
$105,280 = 0.36S
Sales = $292,444.44 ≈ $292,445.

Alternative method:

Note that Sales – VC – FC = EBIT. Calculate net income from EPS and shares outstanding and work back up the income statement.

$EPS_1 = [(EBIT - Interest)(1 - T)]/$Shares outstanding.

Solve for net income, then EBT, interest (step 1 above), and EBIT.

Net Income = EPS × Shares outstanding = $4.00 × 10,000 = $40,000.

EBT = NI/(1 – T) = $40,000/0.6 = $66,667.

Interest (from above) = $28,800.

EBIT = EBT + Interest = $66,667 + $28,800 = $95,467.

Solve for sales using VC percentage, EBIT, and FC.

$$S = 0.40S + \$95,467 + \$80,000$$
$$0.6S = \$175,467$$
$$S = \$175,467/0.6 = \$292,445.$$

13-3. F = $900,000; VC = $3.25/unit; P = $4.75; Q_{BE} = ?

$$Q_{BE} = \frac{F}{P - V}$$
$$= \frac{\$900,000}{\$4.75 - \$3.25}$$
$$= 600,000 \text{ units.}$$

13-4. Facts as given: Current capital structure: 30% D; 70% E; k_{RF} = 6%; $k_M - k_{RF}$ = 5%; T = 40%; k_s = 12%.

Step 1: Determine the firm's current beta.

$$k_s = k_{RF} + (k_M - k_{RF})b$$
$$12\% = 6\% + (5\%)b$$
$$6\% = 5\%b$$
$$1.2 = b.$$

Step 2: Determine the firm's unlevered beta, b_U.

$$b_U = b/[1 + (1 - T)(D/E)]$$
$$b_U = 1.2/[1 + (1 - 0.4)(0.30/0.70)]$$
$$b_U = 1.2/1.2571$$
$$b_U = 0.9545.$$

Step 3: Determine the firm's beta under the new capital structure.

$$b = b_U[1 + (1 - T)(D/E)]$$
$$b = 0.9545[1 + (1 - 0.4)(0.45/0.55)]$$
$$b = 0.9545(1.4909)$$
$$b = 1.4231.$$

Step 4: Determine the firm's new cost of equity under the changed capital structure.

$$k_s = k_{RF} + (k_M - k_{RF})b$$
$$k_s = 6\% + (5\%)1.4231$$
$$k_s = 13.1157\% \approx 13.12\%.$$

CHAPTER 14

14-1. b.

14-2. e. The dividend irrelevance theory is MM's theory. The tax preference theory says that capital gains are preferred to dividends, while the bird-in-the-hand (G-L) theory says that dividends are preferred to capital gains. The clientele effect assumes that investors are attracted to a firm's particular dividend payout policy.

14-3. *Calculate the amount of debt and interest expense (in millions).*

Total assets = $200; 40% debt × $200 = $80 debt.

Interest expense = $80 × 0.10 = $8.

Calculate net income (in millions).

EBIT	$98.0
Less: Interest	8.0
EBT	$90.0
Less: Taxes (@34%)	30.6
Net income	$59.4

Calculate portion of projects financed with retained earnings.

Capital budget consists of $60 million in positive NPV projects.

Retained earnings portion: $60M × 0.60 = $36 million
Debt portion: $60M × 0.40 = $24 million

Calculate residual available for dividends.

$59.4 − $36.0 = $23.4 million in dividends.

CHAPTER 15

15-1. **Time line:**

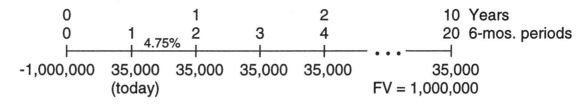

Financial calculator solution:

Calculate the market value of the bonds, V_B, today, at $t = 1$, on the time line above using the new market interest rate.

Inputs: N = 19; I = 9.5/2 = 4.75; PMT = 35000; FV = 1000000.
Output: PV = −$845,807.80.

Calculate the capital loss on the bonds.

The bonds were purchased at par for $1,000,000, but are resold 6 months later for considerably less.

Capital loss on bonds = $1,000,000 − $845,807.80 = $154,192.20.

15-2. d.

15-3. c.

15-4. Construct a simplified comparative balance sheet and income statement for the restricted and relaxed policies (in thousands):

	15% of Sales Restricted	25% of Sales Relaxed
Balance sheet accounts:		
Current assets	$ 60	$ 100
Fixed assets	100	100
Total assets	$ 160	$ 200
Debt	$ 80	$ 100
Equity and retained earnings	80	100
Total liabilities and equity	$ 160	$ 200
Income statement accounts:		
EBIT	$ 36.0	$ 36.0
Less: Interest (10%)	8.0	10.0
EBT	$ 28.0	$ 26.0
Less: Taxes (40%)	11.2	10.4
Net income	$ 16.8	$ 15.6

Calculate ROEs under each policy.

ROE = NI/Equity.
ROE (Restricted policy) = $16.8/$80 = 21.0%.
ROE (Relaxed policy) = $15.6/$100 = 15.6%.
Difference in ROEs = 0.21 − 0.156 = 0.054 = 5.4%.

15-5. (Account balances stated in millions)

Old	With Change

Inventory conversion period:

$$ICP = \frac{365}{\frac{40}{10}} = \frac{365}{4} = 91.25.$$ $$ICP = \frac{365}{\frac{40}{8}} = \frac{365}{5} = 73.$$

Receivables conversion period (or days sales outstanding):

$$DSO = \frac{8}{\frac{40}{365}} = 73.$$ $$DSO = \frac{7}{\frac{40}{365}} = 63.875$$

Payables deferral period:
PDP = 30 days = -30   PDP = -30

CCC = 91.25 + 73 − 30 = 134.25 days.   CCC = 73 + 63.875 − 30 = 106.875 days.